Minnesota Bucket List Adventure Guide

Explore 100 Offbeat Destinations You Must Visit!

Stephen Campbell

Canyon Press
canyon@purplelink.org

Please consider writing a review!
Just visit: purplelink.org/review

ISBN: 978-1-957590-11-0

FREE BONUS

Discover 31 Incredible Places You Can
Visit Next! Just Go To:

purplelink.org/travel

Table of Contents:

Moorhead
New London
Park Rapids
Pipestone
Rochester

How to Use This Book

Welcome to your very own adventure guide to exploring the many wonders of the state of Minnesota. Not only does this book offer the most wonderful places to visit and sights to see in the vast state, but it provides GPS coordinates for Google Maps to make exploring that much easier.

Adventure Guide

Sorted by region, this guide offers over 100 amazing wonders found in Minnesota for you to see and explore. They can be visited in any order and this book will help you keep track of where you've been and where to look forward to going next. Each section describes the area or place, what to look for, physical address, and what you may need to bring along.

GPS Coordinates

As you can imagine, not all of the locations in this book have a physical address. Fortunately, some of our listed wonders are either located within a National Park or Reserve, or near a city, town, or place of business. For those that are not associated with a specific location, it is easiest to map it using GPS coordinates.

Luckily, Google has a system of codes that converts the coordinates into pin-drop locations that Google Maps can interpret and navigate.

Each adventure in this guide includes GPS coordinates along with a physical address whenever it is available.

It is important that you are prepared for poor cell signals. It is recommended that you route your location and ensure that the directions are accessible offline. Depending on your device and the distance of some locations, you may need to travel with a backup battery source.

About Minnesota

Minnesota is known for its many natural lakes, giving the state its nickname of the "Land of 10,000 Lakes." Minnesota's name comes from the Dakota word "mni sota," which translates to "clear water."

Minnesota has been inhabited since at least the eleventh century BCE, with the Dakota people of the Sioux tribe having lived in the area. Modern settlements were first established in 1805 after Zebulon Pike acquired land for the construction of Fort Snelling in the area that would soon become St. Paul, the state's future capital.

Minnesota would become the country's thirty-second state on May 11, 1858. Its agriculture and iron mining industries made the state essential to the nation. Today, Minnesota is a major contributor to the nation's economy, with prominent companies like 3M, UnitedHealth Group, Target, General Mills, and Hormel all operating from there. The state is also home to the Mayo Clinic, one of the world's most-recognized hospitals.

Landscape and Climate

Minnesota is the country's twelfth-largest state, with nearly 87,000 square miles of space. There are nearly 12,000 natural lakes of at least ten acres in size. The portion of Lake Superior within Minnesota is the largest at nearly one million acres. Lake of the Woods and the Rainy, Lower and Upper Red, Mille Lacs, and Leech Lakes are among the state's most massive lakes.

The western parts of the state host a prairie landscape, while the southeast features an eastern broadleaf forest that it shares with Wisconsin. A boreal forest area with spruce and pine trees appears in the north.

Minnesota is home to such wildlife as the elk, caribou, bison, and whitetail deer. It also has one of the country's largest timber wolf and bald eagle populations outside of Alaska. The bass, walleye, pike, trout, and brook are among the most common fish found in the lakes open for fishing throughout the state.

Most of Minnesota features a warm-summer humid continental climate, while parts of the south have a hot-summer humid continental climate. Temperatures often reach the 80s in the summer, while the evenings can reach the 50s. Temperatures are freezing through most of the winter, with conditions reaching up to 25 in the daytime and as low as zero at night. Readings in the northern part of the state are typically ten degrees colder than in the south.

Minnesota receives about 50 inches of snowfall and 30 inches of rainfall each year on average. December and January are the snowiest months.

The northern end of the Mississippi River flows through the state. The Mississippi and St. Croix Rivers form much of the eastern border, while the Red River makes up part of the western border.

Minnesota's population consists of about 5.7 million people as of 2020. Nearly 3.6 million people live in the Twin Cities metropolitan area, which includes the cities of Minneapolis, St. Paul, Bloomington, Brooklyn Park, and Eden Prairie. Other well-known cities in the state include

Rochester, Duluth, St. Cloud, Moorhead, and International Falls.

The state houses eleven Native American reservations, primarily in the northern area. The Red Lake, White Earth, and Grand Portage reservations are the largest in Minnesota.

Minnesota shares borders with North and South Dakota, Iowa, and Wisconsin. There are also seven border crossings between Minnesota and Canada, with three in the east entering Ontario and four in the west leading to Manitoba.

North River Trail & Prairie Loop, Afton State Park

The North River Trail and Prairie Loop is a 7.2-mile hiking loop at Afton State Park in Hastings, a Washington County town off the St. Croix River. The trail follows the river overlooking the border with Wisconsin. It provides many prairie views and features many spots for deer sightings. The trail is open for cross-country skiing during the winter. Some parts of the trail are also open for horseback riding.

Best Time to Visit:
The trail is easy to travel along from March to October.

Pass/Permit/Fees:
Access is free, but it may cost extra for you to rent equipment. You'd have to bring your horse if you want to ride down the trail and adhere to all guidelines and restrictions.

Closest City or Town:
Afton

Physical Address:
6959 Peller Ave S, Hastings, MN 55033

GPS Coordinates:
44.85403 ° N, 92.78651 ° W

Did You Know?
The Afton name comes from a poem about the River Afton in Scotland by Robert Burns.

Spam Museum

Explore the world of the iconic Spam processed meat product at the Spam Museum in Austin, near the headquarters of Hormel Foods, the company that introduced Spam in 1937. The museum includes a look at how Spam is prepared and how it has evolved with multiple varieties. It includes historical displays showcasing Spam's role in food and culture. You'll also find some displays showing how Spam is offered and marketed in countries throughout the world. Visitors can also see how people have used Spam cans for many purposes over the years as well as a section that shows how many cans of Spam they can stack at a time.

Best Time to Visit:
The museum is open throughout the year.

Pass/Permit/Fees:
The museum is free to visit.

Closest City or Town:
Austin

Physical Address:
101 3rd Ave NE, Austin, MN 55912

GPS Coordinates:
43.66943 ° N, 92.97462 ° W

Did You Know?
Hormel sells at least 120 million cans of Spam each year. The product is especially popular in Hawaii and other places where its long shelf-life and easy storage is beneficial.

Lake Bemidji State Park

You will find the Lake Bemidji State Park on the northern end of the lake across from the city of Bemidji. The park includes a portion of the Paul Bunyan State Trail. You can see many plants along the water on the Bog Walk hiking trail. You can also find some birds throughout the area, with gulls and ospreys appearing near the lakeshore. The park has a historic shelter building from 1939 with a rustic look and simulated log cabin design.

Best Time to Visit:
The park hosts eleven miles of cross-country skiing trails during the winter season. You can also take a snowmobile out on three miles of snowmobile trail. Snowshoeing is open throughout most of the park in the winter as well, although you cannot bring snowshoes on groomed trails.

Pass/Permit/Fees:
The park is free to visit, but it costs extra to rent snowshoes or to reserve a camping site.

Closest City or Town:
Bemidji

Physical Address:
3401 State Park Rd NE, Bemidji, MN 56601

GPS Coordinates:
47.53465 ° N, 94.82264 ° W

Did You Know?
Bemidji comes from an Ojibwe word for "lake with crossing waters."

Paul Bunyan State Trail

The Paul Bunyan State Trail is one of the longest recreational trails in the state. It goes between the Crow Wing State Park in Brainerd and the Lake Bemidji State Park in Bemidji. The trail is 115 miles long and has many paved roads for cycling. It is also open for in-line skating, mountain biking, and snowmobiling. The trail goes north from Brainerd through many small towns, many of which feature camping and picnic sites. There are also separate offshoots on the trail that lead to Cass Lake and Park Rapids.

Best Time to Visit:
The trail is easy to traverse during the winter season. You can use studded tracks on the trail if you wish.

Pass/Permit/Fees:
You will require a snowmobile state trail sticker on your snowmobile if you want to use it on the Paul Bunyan trail or any other trail in the state.

Closest City or Town:
North End: Bemidji

Physical Address:
Crow Wing State Park in Brainerd to Lake Bemidji State Park in Bemidji

GPS Coordinates:
North End: 47.53477 ° N, 94.82421 ° W

Did You Know?
You can reach the Mississippi River Trail from Brainerd while on the Paul Bunyan Trail.

The Mall of America

The Mall of America in the southern Minneapolis suburb of Bloomington is the largest shopping mall in the Western Hemisphere. The mall has about 5.6 million square feet of gross leasable area. It offers more than 500 stores on four floors. In addition to shopping, you will find many attractions at the Mall of America. The Sea Life Minnesota Aquarium features hundreds of fish and other forms of marine life on display. The Nickelodeon Universe theme park has amusement rides and games for the whole family. The Crayola Experience shows how crayons are made and features various interactive exhibits. You'll also find many full-service restaurants at the mall.

Best Time to Visit:
The Christmas season is an immensely popular time.

Pass/Permit/Fees:
The mall is free to visit, but charges for each attraction will vary.

Closest City or Town:
Bloomington

Physical Address:
60 E Broadway, Bloomington, MN 55425

GPS Coordinates:
44.85571 ° N, 93.24177 ° W

Did You Know?
The Mall of America is on the old site of Metropolitan Stadium, the former home of the Minnesota Twins and Vikings.

Brainerd International Raceway

Brainerd International Raceway is one of the world's top drag racing sites. The racing complex hosts a 0.25-mile dragstrip for drag racing and car events, with some vehicles traveling close to 300 miles per hour on the strip. The raceway also features two separate road courses and a kart-racing track. The venue hosts many auto races throughout the year, including sports car and motorcycle races. There's a driving school at the raceway where you can learn how to drive a racing car.

Best Time to Visit:
The raceway hosts the Lucas Oil NHRA Nationals every August. The event is one of the world's top drag racing competitions. The nationals bring the world's best dragster, sportsman car, and other car drivers to Brainerd.

Pass/Permit/Fees:
Ticket prices will vary by each event. You can also attend a driving school class here, but it costs at least $400 to enroll in a one-day session.

Closest City or Town:
Brainerd

Physical Address:
5523 Birchdale Rd, Brainerd, MN 56401

GPS Coordinates:
46.41766 ° N, 94.28496 ° W

Did You Know?
In 2005, a driver completed a quarter-mile drag race here at a speed of nearly 338 miles per hour.

Crow Wing County Historical Society Museum and Library

Crow Wing County, in the middle part of the state, has an extensive history presented at the Crow Wing County Historical Society Museum. The group operates its museum inside an early-twentieth-century home. The three-floor museum has exhibits on the railroad industry, the lumber and mining fields, and what home life was like during the turn of the century. The museum also features a library with copies of local newspapers and government reports. Many of these go back to the late nineteenth century, making it a useful site for genealogical research.

Best Time to Visit:
The museum is open from Tuesday to Saturday each week.

Pass/Permit/Fees:
A $3 donation is encouraged for each person.

Closest City or Town:
Brainerd

Physical Address:
320 Laurel St, Brainerd, MN 56401

GPS Coordinates:
46.35581 ° N, 94.20399 ° W

Did You Know?
The property the museum is on belonged to the local sheriff in the early twentieth century. It was also used as a jail building.

Gull Lake

Gull Lake is north of Brainerd and is a popular vacation and recreation spot. Gull Lake Dam was the final Mississippi Headwaters reservoir dam, beginning service in 1912. The site is significant in archaeology due to the presence of 12 burial mounds and partial mounds under the dam. The area has since evolved into a popular resort area with various resorts and boating spaces all around. Gull Lake is open for boating and fishing throughout the spring and summer seasons. There are also a few golf courses near the waterway.

Best Time to Visit:
The lake hosts the Brainerd Ice Fishing Extravaganza every winter with thousands of ice fishing holes prepared on the lake's surface.

Pass/Permit/Fees:
You can visit for free, but the cost to stay at one of the resorts or camping sites around the lake will vary by venue.

Closest City or Town:
Brainerd

Physical Address:
10867 East Gull Lake Dr, Brainerd, MN 56401

GPS Coordinates:
46.42782 ° N, 94.36337 ° W

Did You Know?
These mounds date back to at least 200 AD.

Mille Lacs Lake

Mille Lacs Lake is one of the largest in Minnesota, covering about 130,000 acres of land. But the lake is relatively shallow, as the deepest spot here is about 42 feet. Mille Lacs offers several resorts on all sides, towns like Wahkon and Vineland to the south. The Grand Casino Mille Lacs is to the west and is one of the more popular recreational sites at the lake. People looking for things to do on the water will find plenty of fishing activities here, including reef-top fishing near the shores. Angling and ice fishing are also popular.

Best Time to Visit:
The lake houses thousands of ice fishing houses during the winter season.

Pass/Permit/Fees:
While fishing is accessible to all, you will require a license to fish before you arrive.

Closest City or Town:
Brainerd

Physical Address:
Tourism Council, 42099 State Hwy 47, Isle, MN 56342

GPS Coordinates:
46.23611 ° N, 93.63235 ° W

Did You Know?
Mille Lacs is French for "thousand lakes."

Mount Ski Gull

Mount Ski Gull is a skiing and tubing site off Gull Lake north of Brainerd. The mountain offers various trails for skiing during the winter season, including downhill and cross-country skiing activities. The tubing hill also provides a fast yet gentle ride down-hill in the winter.

You'll also find day hikes and other recreational activities during the summer. The venue hosts outdoor fitness classes and day camps for kids.

Best Time to Visit:
While there are plenty of summer activities here, there are more things to do during the winter months.

Pass/Permit/Fees:
Passes are available for $130 per season. Daily tickets are also available, although the cost will vary.

Closest City or Town:
Brainerd

Physical Address:
9898 County 77 Southwest, Nisswa, MN 56468

GPS Coordinates:
46.44777 ° N, 94.37773 ° W

Did You Know?
The resort offers a skiing school for novices.

Northland Arboretum

The Northland Arboretum is a 580-acre nature reserve with woodland wildflowers growing throughout the landscape. You will also find many native forms of prairie vegetation, including blue-eye grass and pasque flowers.

The arboretum also provides nearly fifteen miles of trail for hiking. Part of the trail goes across an arched bridge that overlooks a local pond.

Best Time to Visit:
The arboretum is open for cross-country skiing in the winter. Some of the trail parts are lit for evening activities.

Pass/Permit/Fees:
Admission is $5 for adults and $1 for kids. Snowshoe rentals are available during the winter.

Closest City or Town:
Brainerd

Physical Address:
14250 Conservation Dr, Baxter, MN 56425

GPS Coordinates:
46.35948 ° N, 94.22789 ° W

Did You Know?
The red pine trees are among the most notable at the arboretum. This tree is also called the Norway pine, as it is similar to some found in Scandinavia.

Safari North Wildlife Park

The Safari North Wildlife Park in Brainerd is a unique zoo that houses many animals you can see up close. The reptiles here include lizards, crocodiles, alligators, and snakes. The birds include the macaw, emu, blue parakeet, and admin stork. Mammals here include various bears, tigers, giraffes, and wolves. You can feed one of the two giraffes, or you can enjoy a camel ride. You can also visit the parakeet exhibit and see the unique ways in which parakeets communicate with humans and each other.

Best Time to Visit:
The park operates a train during the summer months. The train takes people around the habitat and provides unique views of some of the most popular animals in the area.

Pass/Permit/Fees:
Admission is $18 for adults and $13 for kids. Train rides are $5 each; an additional fee may apply for some activities like camel feeding.

Closest City or Town:
Brainerd

Physical Address:
8493 MN-371, Brainerd, MN 56401

GPS Coordinates:
46.27975 ° N, 94.29556 ° W

Did You Know?
The animals at the park represent all six continents.

This Old Farm

This Old Farm is a pioneer village that makes up part of Paul Bunyan Land in Brainerd. The 26-foot talking Paul Bunyan statue is the highlight of this venue.

This Old Farm features many buildings that represent an old village. You'll find a fire station, granary, sawmill, one-room schoolhouse, dentist office, and blacksmith shop here.

The amusement section includes a train ride, a haunted house, and a few kid-friendly rides. The area is heavily inspired by county fairs.

Best Time to Visit:
The farm and park are open in the summer and fall.

Pass/Permit/Fees:
Admission is $22 per person.

Closest City or Town:
Brainerd

Physical Address:
17553 MN-18, Brainerd, MN 56401

GPS Coordinates:
46.35005 ° N, 94.02906 ° W

Did You Know?
Brainerd is one of many cities that claims to be the birthplace of the mythical character Paul Bunyan. Bemidji and Akeley also have similar claims.

Silver Creek Trail, Jay Cooke State Park

The Silver Creek Trail is a 3.4-mile trail that goes through the Jay Cooke State Park. The trail starts at the Swinging Bridge and goes in a loop, with many parts of the trail traveling near the Saint Louis River.

This trail features a mild elevation gain of about 300 feet. You'll find some splendid views of the local forests in the area, with some spots climbing to more than a thousand feet above sea level. You can also see much of the Saint Louis River from the eastern end of the trail.

The trail is easy for people of all skill levels to travel. It is also open for road biking and dog walking.

Best Time to Visit:
The trail is easier to traverse during the summer months.

Pass/Permit/Fees:
There is no cost to visit the trail.

Closest City or Town:
Carlton

Physical Address:
780 MN-210, Carlton, MN 55718

GPS Coordinates:
46.65398 ° N, 92.37270 ° W

Did You Know?
The water tends to flow a little faster around some parts of Silver Creek at the southern end of the trail.

Gooseberry Falls State Park

Gooseberry Falls State Park covers nearly 1,700 acres of land near Lake Superior. The venue features a large waterfall that leads to the Gooseberry River near the western end of the park.

The park has a few hiking spots, including the Gitchi-Gami State Trail and Superior Hiking Trail. It is also popular among birding enthusiasts. You'll find many birds during the warmer times of the year, including the gray jay, American crow, common grackle, and house sparrow.

Best Time to Visit:
You'll be more likely to find some of the birds around the park during the summer and fall seasons. There are few birds here in the winter, although you could spot the red or white-breasted nuthatch or the blue jay during that season.

Pass/Permit/Fees:
You can visit the park for free.

Closest City or Town:
Castle Danger

Physical Address:
Visitor Center, 3206 MN-61, Two Harbors, MN 55616

GPS Coordinates:
47.14368 ° N, 91.46514 ° W

Did You Know?
The park also has a beach open during the summer season. Agate Beach is popular for its secluded atmosphere.

Paisley Park

The rock musician Prince is considered one of Minnesota's most famous performers. His estate in the western Minneapolis suburb of Chanhassen is available for touring. Paisley Park is a 65,000 square-foot complex that hosts a studio where Prince recorded many of his albums. It also has a soundstage where he would rehearse for concerts and prepare various multimedia productions. The mansion holds many artifacts relating to Prince's work. You can see his outfits, guitars, art pieces, and some of his cars and motorcycles. The estate also houses a vault that includes many of his unreleased recordings. His ashes and the Paisley Park-shaped urn they are stored in are in the vault as well.

Best Time to Visit:
The mansion is open year-round, but it is closed on Wednesdays.

Pass/Permit/Fees:
Tours are $45 per person.

Closest City or Town:
Chanhassen

Physical Address:
7801 Audubon Rd, Chanhassen, MN 55317

GPS Coordinates:
44.86174 ° N, 93.56067 ° W

Did You Know?
Paisley Park is managed by the same group that runs Graceland, Elvis Presley's home in Memphis.

The Minnesota Landscape Arboretum

You will find the Minnesota Landscape Arboretum outside
Chanhassen in the western end of the Minneapolis area.
The arboretum has 1,200 acres of land and includes more
than five thousand species of plants.

Many of the plants here are designed for northern climates.
These include annual and perennial plants alike. You can
also look for many birds throughout the area, including
various sparrows, blackbirds, and wood-warblers.

Best Time to Visit:
The plants are mostly in bloom here in the summer. It is
also easier to find a greater variety of birds here in the
summer.

Pass/Permit/Fees:
Admission is $15 for adults.

Closest City or Town:
Chanhassen

Physical Address:
3675 Arboretum Dr, Chaska, MN 55318

GPS Coordinates:
44.86224 ° N, 93.61543 ° W

Did You Know?
Some of the hiking trails around the arboretum are open for
cross-country skiing during the winter months.

R. W. Lindholm Service Station

You can fill up your tank at a gas station in Cloquet that was designed by Frank Lloyd Wright. The R.W. Lindholm Service Station is based on Wright's original design for a city that would rely on automobile travel. He designed a gas station with an observation area and a canopy to create a public meeting space. The station opened in 1958 and is one of the last Wright-designed buildings to open in his lifetime. The station has a lookout tower in the middle and a cantilevered canopy that points towards the St. Louis River. The glass walls in the observation lounge were designed to create a social environment.

Best Time to Visit:
The station is open year-round.

Pass/Permit/Fees:
The gas pumps are functional. Check the sign to see what it costs for fuel before you start pumping. The station still uses classic-style pumps, so you'd have to pay indoors first.

Closest City or Town:
Cloquet

Physical Address:
202 Cloquet Ave, Cloquet, MN 55720

GPS Coordinates:
46.72129 ° N, 92.46085 ° W

Did You Know?
Phillips 66 operated the station for a few years. Some of the inspirations in the Wright station carried over to future Phillips 66 stations, including the canopy layout.

World's Largest Ball of Twine by One Man

It took from 1950 to 1979 for Francis A. Johnson to build one of Minnesota's most interesting and popular sights. The world's largest ball of twine rolled by one man is in Darwin, a town in Meeker County.

Johnson's ball of twine is certified as the largest ball of sisal twine to have been built by one person. It is about 12 feet in diameter and weighs about 17,400 pounds. The ball is inside a gazebo on 1st Street in downtown Darwin.

Best Time to Visit:
Darwin celebrates Twine Ball Day on the second Saturday of August each year.

Pass/Permit/Fees:
The ball is free to visit, but it is kept in a glass enclosure to ensure no one can touch it.

Closest City or Town:
Darwin

Physical Address:
1st St, Darwin, MN 55324

GPS Coordinates:
45.09685 ° N, 94.41009 ° W

Did You Know?
Francis A. Johnson wrapped a ball of twine for four hours each day during its 29-year construction period. It is unclear as to why he built it.

Duluth Aerial Lift Bridge

The Aerial Lift Bridge in Duluth is one of the country's most unique bridges. It is a rare vertical-lift bridge built in 1905 and converted to its current layout in 1930. The structure is part of a canal that links Lake Superior to the St. Louis River. It is about 390 feet long and features a mechanism that allows the bridge to lift 135 feet in the air in about a minute to allow ships to pass through. The bridge connects downtown Duluth with the Park Point Recreation Area to the south. The Superior Entry Lighthouse is also to the south.

Best Time to Visit:
The bridge routinely lifts up and down throughout the day.

Pass/Permit/Fees:
The bridge is free to cross.

Closest City or Town:
Duluth

Physical Address:
601 S Lake Ave, Duluth, MN 55802

GPS Coordinates:
46.78036 ° N, 92.09270 ° W

Did You Know?
This structure was originally a transporter bridge before it was converted to its current format in 1930. A transporter bridge features a gondola-like design that moves cars and people from one end to the other. The vertical bridge layout used today is considered more practical.

Duluth Children's Museum

Your children will enjoy the experience at the Duluth Children's Museum. This museum in downtown Duluth has many exhibits that feature fun ways for kids to play and learn about the local climate and the unique ecosystem in Minnesota.

The museum also has various fun exhibits on sailing and water, including many that involve Lake Superior. Visitors can discover stories about science and how it impacts daily life as well.

Best Time to Visit:
The museum is open from Thursdays to Sundays.

Pass/Permit/Fees:
Admission is $9 per person.

Closest City or Town:
Duluth

Physical Address:
2125 W Superior St, Duluth, MN 55806

GPS Coordinates:
46.76626 ° N, 92.12534 ° W

Did You Know?
The museum hosts annual camps where people can explore different concepts of science and participate in hands-on activities.

Glensheen, The Historic Congdon Estate

The University of Minnesota at Duluth operates the
Glensheen Mansion, a 1908 estate once owned by
prominent capitalist Chester Adgate Congdon. The
Jacobean Revival property has thirty-nine rooms to explore.

The Jacobean Revival design showcases many influences
from around the world, including Art Nouveau and
Victorian styles. You'll find Japanese silk embroidery and
many authentic American paintings throughout the estate.
There's also an old boathouse near the estate that overlooks
Lake Superior.

Best Time to Visit:
The venue hosts many Christmas activities during the
holiday season. It is adorned with extensive Christmas
decorations as well.

Pass/Permit/Fees:
Admission is $20 for adults.

Closest City or Town:
Duluth

Physical Address:
3300 London Rd, Duluth, MN 55804

GPS Coordinates:
46.81573 ° N, 92.05188 ° W

Did You Know?
Many of the pieces of furniture at the mansion date back to
the 1900s. These include items that are still in the same
spots they were at when the building first opened.

Great Lakes Aquarium

The Great Lakes Aquarium in Duluth has more than 250 species of fish and marine life on display. The aquarium's Isle Royale tank features about 85,000 gallons of water and covers the first and second floors of the aquarium. You can see the fish from many angles throughout the aquarium body. The aquarium has an exhibit on the Saint Louis River, and visitors can see many native species of fish on display here, including the perch, sturgeon, and walleye. The Otter Cover is also popular, as it houses a few North American river otters. The aquarium has a pool with various forms of sturgeon from around the world, from Florida to Russia.

Best Time to Visit:
Visit glaquarium.org to see what the latest rotating exhibits are.

Pass/Permit/Fees:
Admission is $16 for adults and $13 for kids.

Closest City or Town:
Duluth

Physical Address:
353 Harbor Dr #100, Duluth, MN 55802

GPS Coordinates:
46.77930 ° N, 92.10039 ° W

Did You Know?
Other exhibits at the aquarium include ones about invasive species and how they work, a birds of prey exhibit, and a look at freshwater creatures.

Hartley Nature Center

The Hartley Nature Center in the northern end of Duluth has many spaces for hiking and cycling. Some of the trails lead to Hartley Pond and Tischer Creek in the middle, while others go towards Rock Knob, a small overlook.

The nature center building offers exhibits on the unique wildlife and plants found throughout the northern Minnesota area. The area also includes details on conservation efforts throughout the region.

Best Time to Visit:
While the trails and the nature center building are open throughout the week, most of the activities here take place on weekends. These include various nature play activities for kids.

Pass/Permit/Fees:
While you can visit for free, donations are accepted.

Closest City or Town:
Duluth

Physical Address:
3001 Woodland Ave, Duluth, MN 55803

GPS Coordinates:
46.83840 ° N, 92.08266 ° W

Did You Know?
The nature center is open for cross-country skiing during the winter season. There are three difficulty levels available, along with multiple contours around the area.

Hawk Ridge Bird Observatory

You will find many birds of prey at the Hawk Ridge Bird Observatory in Duluth, including such distinct birds as the osprey, turkey vulture, bald eagle, red-tailed hawk, peregrine falcon, and merlin.

The observatory studies the migration of birds of prey and reviews how they can travel over large bodies of water, including nearby Lake Superior. You can join in and see many of the birds as they travel through one of the various trails at the observatory.

Best Time to Visit:
Most of the migration activities here occur from August to November. September is the busiest month for migrations and spotting.

Pass/Permit/Fees:
The observatory does not charge admission, although donations are encouraged.

Closest City or Town:
Duluth

Physical Address:
3980 E Skyline Pkwy, Duluth, MN 55804

GPS Coordinates:
46.84700 ° N, 92.03166 ° W

Did You Know?
The raptor migration counts at the observatory have been consistent over the past few years. The venue counts about 50,000 total raptors each migratory season.

Jay Cooke State Park

The Jay Cooke State Park is southwest of Duluth and is near the northwestern end of Wisconsin. The park features a swinging bridge that goes over the nearby St. Louis River. There are many red clay sediments formed from glaciation. You'll also find a few historic rustic cabins throughout the park area. These include cabins used for plumbing and recreational needs. At least 150 bird species can be found including the great blue heron.

Best Time to Visit:
You'll have an easier time looking for birds here during the fall season.

Pass/Permit/Fees:
There is no admission fee for this park.

Closest City or Town:
Duluth

Physical Address:
780 MN-210, Carlton, MN 55718

GPS Coordinates:
46.65193 ° N, 92.34673 ° W

Did You Know?
The park is a popular site for geocaching. This activity entails people using navigational efforts to find containers hidden in some spots.

Lake Superior Maritime Visitor Center

The Lake Superior Maritime Visitor Center is north of the Aerial Lift Bridge in Duluth. The Army Corps of Engineers operates the venue. The museum hosts exhibits about the history of maritime operations around Lake Superior. It includes models, equipment, and other devices surrounding the marine industry and travel in the region.

There are more than fifty models on display here, with each showing different boat designs from history. There's also a segment in the museum highlighting the construction of the Aerial Lift Bridge, how it works, and its value.

Best Time to Visit:
The museum is open year-round.

Pass/Permit/Fees:

Closest City or Town:
Duluth

Physical Address:
600 Canal Park Dr, Duluth, MN 55802

GPS Coordinates:
46.77991 ° N, 92.09228 ° W

Did You Know?
You can see a three-story-tall steam engine inside the venue.

Lake Superior Railroad Museum

The first floor of the Duluth Union Depot includes the Lake Superior Railroad Museum. The museum houses various locomotives and railcars from history.

Locomotives here include steam, electric, and diesel models, with some dating to the late nineteenth century. Some of the locomotives remain operational. There are also various passenger cars on display from Chicago and Northwestern, Canadian National, and Great Northern.

Best Time to Visit:
You can visit lsrm.org for details on what locomotives are currently on display. The listing changes during the year.

Pass/Permit/Fees:
Museum admission is $12 for adults and $6 for kids.

Closest City or Town:
Duluth

Physical Address:
506 W Michigan St, Duluth, MN 55802

GPS Coordinates:
46.78100 ° N, 92.10399 ° W

Did You Know?
Many of the locomotives on display were donated by their former operators. These include a few that were operating as late as the early twenty-first century.

Lake Superior Zoo & Zoological Society

The Lake Superior Zoo in Duluth includes many exhibits highlighting animals from the north. You will find exhibits that showcase bears, prairie dogs, and many others here. The zoo also has a bald eagle exhibit as well as habitats for lions and even turtles.

Many replicated environments highlight where these animals can be found in the wild. The zoo also hosts regular talks with the keepers who care for these animals.

Best Time to Visit:
The zoo is open year-round.

Pass/Permit/Fees:
Admission for adults is $14, while kids will pay $7.

Closest City or Town:
Duluth

Physical Address:
7210 Fremont St, Duluth, MN 55807

GPS Coordinates:
46.72583 ° N, 92.19050 ° W

Did You Know?
The elephant house at the zoo has been in operation since 1937.

Marshall W. Alworth Planetarium

The Marshall W. Alworth Planetarium is on the campus of
the University of Minnesota in Duluth. The planetarium
hosts public shows that present the evening sky and
showcases various stars and other celestial bodies. There
are programs about how many constellations and other
patterns have been found by people and their different
meanings. These include Greek constellations and many
legends established by Native Americans.

Best Time to Visit:
The most popular events here occur in the evening hours.

Pass/Permit/Fees:
Most of the sessions here are free, but it may cost extra to
participate in some activities.

Closest City or Town:
Duluth

Physical Address:
1023 University Dr, Duluth, MN 55812

GPS Coordinates:
46.81568 ° N, 92.08700 ° W

Did You Know?
The planetarium's location is in an area where outside
lights will not be a concern, making it easier for you to see
the sky.

Park Point

Park Point is a sand spit that stretches out from Duluth and is about seven miles long. The point starts on the southern end of the Aerial Lift Bridge.

Park Point has a recreation area in the middle. It includes a small beach area, plus a dock for boating.

The Park Point Trail goes south from the recreation area to the tip of the point. You will go past the Zero Point Lighthouse, and end at the Superior Entry Channel between Minnesota and Wisconsin.

Best Time to Visit:
You can visit the point at any time of the year.

Pass/Permit/Fees:
The point is free to enter.

Closest City or Town:
Duluth

Physical Address:
5000 Minnesota Ave, Duluth, MN 55802

GPS Coordinates:
46.77516 ° N, 92.09148 ° W

Did You Know?
Park Point can be considered an island since the Duluth Ship Canal separates the point from the rest of the state.

Skyline Parkway

You will see the beautiful scenes of Duluth on the Skyline Parkway. The road is a path that starts in the southern end of Duluth and continues north near historic Highway 61. The parkway links to local sites like Bardon's Peak, the Stewart Creek Bridge, the Oneota Overlook, and Twin Ponds. You can view downtown Duluth from many parts of the parkway, including prime views of the Aerial Lift Bridge. It eventually leads to the shore of Lake Superior near Highway 61 at the northern end.

Best Time to Visit:
The fall season is an amazing time, as the natural yellow and orange colors of the leaves will be on full display.

Pass/Permit/Fees:
You can reach the parkway at any time with no tolls necessary.

Closest City or Town:
Duluth

Physical Address:
2949 W Skyline Pkwy, Duluth, MN 55810

GPS Coordinates:
46.72849 ° N, 92.20648 ° W

Did You Know?
The parkway makes its way around many golf courses. The Northland Country Club in the middle part of the parkway is the city's most popular one. You'll also find the Enger Park Golf Course to the west.

Spirit Mountain

Spirit Mountain has outdoor activities for people outside Duluth to enjoy year-round. You can ride the Timber Twister elevated track ride in the summer or jump up and down on the Jumping Pillow. There's also a disc golf course and a nine-hole miniature golf course here. Mountain biking is open in the summer. You'll find trails for all skill levels around the area, including a hiking trail in the middle part of the mountain. Skiing and snow tubing are popular winter activities.

Best Time to Visit:
Any time of year.

Pass/Permit/Fees:
Prices will vary throughout the year. Lift tickets in the winter are $65 for adults and $49 for kids. Tickets for summer activities cost $49 each. It also costs between $9 and $14 for chairlift rides.

Closest City or Town:
Duluth

Physical Address:
9500 Spirit Mountain Pl, Duluth, MN 55810

GPS Coordinates:
46.71833 ° N, 92.21659 ° W

Did You Know?
The average highs in Duluth in the winter will reach around 15 degrees. Dress accordingly if you plan to visit in the winter.

SS William A. Irvin

The *SS William A. Irvin* is a lake freighter open for tours in Duluth. She is docked northwest of the Aerial Lift Bridge. The ship is named after the former U.S. Steel president. It has a distinct red hull and is about 610 feet long, featuring a straight deck design with no self-unloading system. Visitors can tour the ship and see what boat life was like when the ship was built in 1938. You can visit the kitchen, the living quarters, and various storage spaces as well as see how items were loaded in the cargo area, which could fit 14,000 tons of materials.

Best Time to Visit:
The ship is open year-round, but in October the ship hosts Haunted Ship events.

Pass/Permit/Fees:
Admission onboard is $15 for adults and $10 for military members.

Closest City or Town:
Duluth

Physical Address:
350 Harbor Dr, Duluth, MN 55802

GPS Coordinates:
46.78281 ° N, 92.09721 ° W

Did You Know?
The *SS William A. Irvin* is referred to with female pronouns like any other ship. This point comes from the belief in a mother figure or goddess protecting a ship and her crew.

Tweed Museum of Art

The University of Minnesota at Duluth houses the Tweed Museum of Art. The museum has a thorough collection of American and European art. It holds one of the largest collections of landscape art in the country, including a thorough collection of works by American artist Gilbert Munger. The Tweed Museum includes a vast selection of pieces from American Indian artists. These include many works from people in the Eastern Woodlands. Many of these pieces have been on display at the National Museum of the American Indian in Washington.

Best Time to Visit:
The museum hosts many exhibitions throughout the year, including select events that include works by UMD students. Check with the campus to see what is there before visiting.

Pass/Permit/Fees:
Admission is $5 for a family or $2 for individuals.

Closest City or Town:
Duluth

Physical Address:
1201 Ordean Ct, Duluth, MN 55812

GPS Coordinates:
46.81858 ° N, 92.08439 ° W

Did You Know?
The museum's collection started in 1950 following a donation of hundreds of pieces of art that belonged to a local citizen.

United States Hockey Hall of Fame

The United States Hockey Hall of Fame in Eveleth is a museum honoring the development of ice hockey in the country. The museum includes exhibits and artifacts from the development of hockey, with many items dating back to the early twentieth century.

There is a hall of fame that honors many famous American hockey stars. It also features exhibits on many American Olympic hockey teams, including the gold-medal-winning men's 1960 and 1980 teams and the women's 1998 team.

Best Time to Visit:
The Hall of Fame traditionally holds its annual induction ceremony late in the year.

Pass/Permit/Fees:
Admission is $8 for adults and $6 for kids.

Closest City or Town:
Eveleth

Physical Address:
801 Hat Trick Ave, Eveleth, MN 55734

GPS Coordinates:
47.47165 ° N, 92.52833 ° W

Did You Know?
You'll also find the world's largest regulation hockey stick on display in downtown Eveleth. The stick is about 110 feet long.

Boundary Waters Canoe Area

The Boundary Waters Canoe Area is in the heart of the Superior National Forest. You'll find dozens of canoe and kayak entry points throughout the region. You can paddle your way through some of the many lakes, including the Trout, Crooked, Snowbank, and Fall Lakes. You'll find nearly a million acres of land here with wolves, deer, moose, beavers, and bald eagles around the water. The region also has various igneous and metamorphic rocks formed thousands of years ago.

Best Time to Visit:
The canoe area is the easiest to visit from May to September.

Pass/Permit/Fees:
You will require a permit to enter the canoe area. You must enter the designated entry point on the specific date your permit lists.

Closest City or Town:
Ely

Physical Address:
Superior National Forest, Duluth, MN 55808

GPS Coordinates:
47.91463 ° N, 91.85760 ° W

Did You Know?
Woodland caribou sightings are rare. The deer population has forced many caribou from the area. A brain worm parasite transmitted by deer to caribous has also been a concern.

Burntside Lake, Saint Louis County

Burntside Lake is one of the most popular water spots in the northern end of Minnesota. The lake is in Saint Louis County near Ely. Burntside Lake is open for kayaking and canoeing, so you can go near one of the more than one hundred islands scattered around the water. The area is home to the Burntside Lodge and Camp Van Vac, two resorts that have been operating since the 1910s, with various log cabins and multiple docks for boats. You can also go fishing throughout the lake for bluegill, walleye, yellow perch, and lake trout.

Best Time to Visit:
The weather conditions are most comfortable in the summer.

Pass/Permit/Fees:
You can reserve a room at one of the resorts on the lake, but the cost will vary.

Closest City or Town:
Ely

Physical Address:
Public water access is found just past 3321 Wolf Lake Rd, Ely, MN 55731

GPS Coordinates:
47.92071 ° N, 91.95511 ° W

Did You Know?
A few of the islands in the lake are Scientific and Natural Areas for study through the support of the Nature Conservancy.

Dorothy Molter Museum

The Dorothy Molter Museum showcases the unique history and stories of northeastern Minnesota. The museum has collections showcasing the many discoveries people have made while in the area. The museum also has exhibits on the Isle of Pines and how people would enjoy off-grid living and exploration around its many lakes. It also features various forms of wildlife found in the area over the years.

Best Time to Visit:
The summer season is an enjoyable time to visit, as winter conditions can be difficult.

Pass/Permit/Fees:
The museum is free to visit. The place also has root beer-related products for sale. You can order a copy of Dorothy Molter's root beer recipe for $3.

Closest City or Town:
Ely

Physical Address:
2002 E Sheridan St, Ely, MN 55731

GPS Coordinates:
47.90301 ° N, 91.83390 ° W

Did You Know?
The namesake of the museum was a popular figure in the Ely area. Dorothy Molter lived there for nearly fifty years and would often make root beer and serve it to canoeists going through.

International Wolf Center

The International Wolf Center in Ely studies wolf
populations and explores their relationship to the wild. You
will learn about the biology and behavior of wolves and
about the many types of wolves you can find in the wild.
You can explore how gray and red wolves are different and
how they relate to the domestic dog. The International Wolf
Center also has a wolf habitat that includes a few wolves on
display. The center helps take care of many wolves, and
helps support wolf pups as they grow.

Best Time to Visit:
The center's wolf exhibit and pup logs will change
throughout the year. Visit wolf.org to learn more about
what is happening here and what is on display.

Pass/Permit/Fees:
Admission is $14 for adults and $8 for kids.

Closest City or Town:
Ely

Physical Address:
1396 MN-169, Ely, MN 55731

GPS Coordinates:
47.90624 ° N, 91.82767 ° W

Did You Know?
The Minnesota Department of Natural Resources estimates
that about 2,700 wolves are living in the wild around the
state as of 2019. The total is more than twice the wolf
population of 1979.

North American Bear Center

Discover the world of bears at the North American Bear Center in Ely. The venue is dedicated to helping people understand bears and their habitats. You can learn about how bears communicate with each other, how they hibernate, reproduce, and forage for food, and what the mothers do when raising their cubs. You'll also learn about many of the myths surrounding bears. The center has exhibits on black, brown, and polar bears, including a habitat where four black bears live. The workers here study these bears and show people how they live in the wild.

Best Time to Visit:
The center is open from June to October. Group visits are available outside that season, although the live bears here might not be visible then.

Pass/Permit/Fees:
Adult admission is $14, while kids can visit for $9.

Closest City or Town:
Ely

Physical Address:
1926 MN-169, Ely, MN 55731

GPS Coordinates:
47.89951 ° N, 91.88825 ° W

Did You Know?
Minnesota has a population of about 12,000 to 15,000 black bears.

Artists Point

Artists Point gets its name from how the picturesque scenes in this area near Grand Marais are worthy of being in a painting. You might find some artists with their easels set up around the rock formations here as they paint the local landscape. Artists Point reveals a beautiful scene with the clear blue water of Lake Superior flowing near the trees and nearby buildings in Grand Marais. The area is also ideal for sailing, as you can reach the nearby Grand Marais Lighthouse by boat. Artists Point includes several small islands near the shore. Many of these islands are easy to reach by walking, as the waters around them aren't too deep.

Best Time to Visit:
You'll see ice forming off the trees and rocks in the winter.

Pass/Permit/Fees:
You can reach the point for free.

Closest City or Town:
Grand Marais

Physical Address:
Co Rd 10, Grand Marais, MN 55604

GPS Coordinates:
47.74550 ° N, 90.33286 ° W

Did You Know?
The United States Coast Guard has a customs and border protection station near Artists Point. The station is about 35 miles southwest of the Canadian border.

Devil's Kettle Falls

Devil's Kettle Falls near Grand Marais is one of the most mysterious waterfalls in Minnesota. The waterfall is in the Brule River and is about a mile north of Lake Superior in Judge CR Magney State Park.

The waterfall splits in the middle, with the eastern side flowing about fifty feet into a nearby pool. It is believed that the water from the west goes underground and eventually reaches Lake Superior. There's also the belief that the western water may reenter the Brule River.

Best Time to Visit:
Visiting conditions are best in the spring and summer.

Pass/Permit/Fees:
You can reach the waterfall for free.

Closest City or Town:
Grand Marais

Physical Address:
Superior Hiking Trail, 4051 MN-61, Grand Marais, MN 55604

GPS Coordinates:
47.82974 ° N, 90.04932 ° W

Did You Know?
Although you could try to drop something in the western end of the waterfall to see where it will come out, that does not work. The pool at the bottom of the western end produces strong recirculating currents that can destroy most material it receives.

Grand Marais Lighthouse

The Grand Marais Lighthouse is in the middle of a breakwater area on the shore of Lake Superior in Grand Marais. The functioning lighthouse was built in 1922 and features a focal height of about 48 feet. It has a square pyramidal skeleton style, and the breakwater is a concrete walkway. Artists Point is where the breakwater begins, across from the lighthouse.

The lighthouse has the original keeper's house on its site, and the site is run by the Cook County Historical Society.

Best Time to Visit:
The lighthouse is open from May to October.

Pass/Permit/Fees:
Admission is $12 for adults.

Closest City or Town:
Grand Marais

Physical Address:
Grand Marais, MN 55604

GPS Coordinates:
47.74523 ° N, 90.33755 ° W

Did You Know?
The lighthouse lens is relatively small, as it is about 0.5 meters high. But the it does project light several miles away, which is necessary for sailing on Lake Superior.

Gunflint Trail

Gunflint Trail is a 56-mile trail that starts in Grand Marais and leads up to Saganaga Lake near the Ontario border to the north. Also known as County Road 12, the trail goes past many forest spaces and waterways formed by glaciers. You will find a variety of flora and fauna along the trail, including the white-tailed deer, moose, black bear, lynx, and wolf. The pine, fir, and spruce trees that line the trail are several centuries old.

Best Time to Visit:
Gunflint Trail is the busiest during the summer season, as that is a popular time for canoeing and fishing.

Pass/Permit/Fees:
While you can travel down the Gunflint Trail for free, it will cost extra to rent a canoe or kayak or to get a fishing license.

Closest City or Town:
Grand Marais

Physical Address:
County Road 12, Grand Marais, MN 55604

GPS Coordinates:
Northern End: 48.15910 ° N, 90.89509 ° W
Southern End: 47.75484 ° N, 90.32454 ° W

Did You Know?
The trail started in the 1890s to reach the Paulson Mine, but it would not be fully completed until the 1970s.

Hungry Jack Lake

Hungry Jack Lake is one of the most intriguing lakes in Minnesota. It is located in the northeastern part of the state and is accessible from the northern part of the Gunflint Trail. The lake is about 460 acres in size and up to 70 feet deep.

Most of the camping sites around the lake are at the western end. The site is popular for fishing, especially as it features many wide-open spots.

Best Time to Visit:
The summer season is an excellent time to visit.

Pass/Permit/Fees:
While it is free to visit the lake, you may need to spend extra to dock a boat here. You'll also require a fishing license if you want to fish while in the area.

Closest City or Town:
Grand Marais

Physical Address:
372 Hungry Jack Rd, Grand Marais, MN 55604

GPS Coordinates:
48.05896 ° N, 90.44506 ° W

Did You Know?
Hungry Jack Lake takes its name from Anderson Jackson Scott, a surveyor's assistant who worked at the lake and had scarce food supplies.

Grand Portage State Park

You will find the state's tallest waterfall at the Grand Portage State Park. The park houses High Falls, a 120-foot waterfall in the middle of an old fur trade route that was used between the United States and Canada.

You can go down Falls Trail to see the waterfall on Pigeon River. The river also indicates the border between Minnesota and Ontario. Pigeon River International Bridge links the U.S. and Canada from some of the eastern parts of the park.

Best Time to Visit:
The waterfall looks its best during the winter season, as the surrounding areas are covered in ice with many icicle formations.

Pass/Permit/Fees:
The park is free to visit; however it does cost to reserve a campsite or to bring an off-roading vehicle to the area.

Closest City or Town:
Grand Portage

Physical Address:
9393 E, MN-61, Grand Portage, MN 55605

GPS Coordinates:
48.00086 ° N, 89.59070 ° W

Did You Know?
The Grand Portage Indian Reservation leases the park to the state for $1 each year. It is the only park that is jointly managed by a tribe and a state.

High Falls

The tallest waterfall in Minnesota is on the Canadian border at the Grand Portage State Park. High Falls is about 120 feet high, with water flowing down to the Pigeon River that divides Minnesota and Ontario.

High Falls is on the northwestern end of the Grand Portage State Park next to the Canadian border. About half of the waterfall is on the American side of the Pigeon River.

Best Time to Visit:
The strongest water flows appear during the spring season. But the winter season is also a beautiful time to see the waterfall as it freezes.

Pass/Permit/Fees:
You can reach the High Falls for free.

Closest City or Town:
Grand Portage

Physical Address:
9393 East Highway 61, Grand Portage, MN 55605

GPS Coordinates:
48.00441 ° N, 89.59761 ° W

Did You Know?
The boundary between Minnesota and Ontario was dictated by the Treaty of Paris in 1783.

Hollow Rock

Hollow Rock is a small natural arch formation off the coast of Lake Superior near Grand Portage. The rock is a few feet from the land and is accessible through a small rock passage to the north. The natural arch in Hollow Rock comes from thousands of years of erosion. The waters of Lake Superior have triggered erosion for centuries, thus leading to this distinct design. The area also features a few small trees on the top that remain intact.

Best Time to Visit:
The evening hours are the best time to visit, as light pollution will not be a problem when looking out at the stars.

Pass/Permit/Fees:
There is no admission to the area.

Closest City or Town:
Grand Portage

Physical Address:
7422 MN-61, Grand Portage, MN 55605

GPS Coordinates:
47.91721 ° N, 89.73630 ° W

Did You Know?
The morning hours are a unique time for the Hollow Rock area, as the fog in the region will flow over the rocks leading to the arch.

Minnesota Highway 61 Scenic Road

Minnesota Highway 61 is a scenic road that starts in the south near I-35 in Duluth and ends at the Canadian border in Grand Portage. The scenic road is about 150 miles long. Highway 61 will take you through many park spaces like Gooseberry Falls, Split Rock Lighthouse, Temperance River, and Grand Portage State Parks. The road also moves through the towns of Schroeder, Tofte, Grand Marais, Red Rock, and Grand Portage. The road then continues into Ontario, ending in the city of Thunder Bay.

Best Time to Visit: The road is open throughout the year, although some sections may not be well-maintained during the winter season.

Pass/Permit/Fees: The road does not charge tolls.

Closest City or Town:
Grand Portage

Physical Address:
Duluth to Grand Portage

GPS Coordinates:
48.00124 ° N, 89.58575 ° W

Did You Know?
Most of Highway 61 is a two-lane highway, although some parts of the road near Duluth have four lanes.

Mount Josephine

The effort to climb up Mount Josephine can be a challenge, but those who make it up to the 1,342-foot summit will be rewarded with outstanding views of Lake Superior and the surroundings around northeastern Minnesota. Mount Josephine is accessible from a 2.5-mile trail that brings you hundreds of feet up in the air. The steep surface and rocky terrain make the mountain hike challenging and unique. You can see the bay and the Teal Lake to the north. You may also see the Pigeon River to the north on a cloudless day. Please keep in mind that the trailhead is notably difficult to find. If you run into issues, seek out local help at the Grand Portage Museum, which is a one-minute walk from the trailhead.

Best Time to Visit: The air is a little clearer during the summer season, so try and visit during that time if possible.

Pass/Permit/Fees: You can reach the area for free.

Closest City or Town:
Grand Portage

Physical Address:
Grand Portage Museum, 54 Upper Rd, Grand Portage, MN 55605

GPS Coordinates:
47.97215° N, 89.66846 ° W

Did You Know?
The trail is open for dog walking. Be sure you keep your dogs in check while on the trail, as the space can be steep for some breeds.

Niagara Cave

Niagara Cave is a 200-foot-deep cave in Fillmore County near the border with Iowa. The cave brings you on a mile-long hike down towards limestone formations and fossils that are nearly 450 million years old. You'll also find a 60-foot waterfall in the middle of the area.

The stalactites and stalagmites around Niagara Cave are among the deepest in the state. There's also a meeting area inside the cave that may have been used as a prehistoric wedding chapel.

Best Time to Visit: The cave is open from April to October each year. Conditions in the cave are 48 degrees throughout the year, so be sure you wear the proper clothing when entering.

Pass/Permit/Fees: Admission is $20 for adults and $12 for kids.

Closest City or Town:
Harmony

Physical Address:
29842 Co Hwy 30, Harmony, MN 55939

GPS Coordinates:
43.51459 ° N, 92.05410 ° W

Did You Know?
The limestone formations have been evolving for centuries, but the cave itself wasn't discovered until 1924.

Smokey Bear Park

Smokey Bear Park in International Falls is a park near the Rainy River that divides Minnesota from Ontario. The park has some picnic areas, and it is home to the Koochiching County Historical Museum.

The park's most prominent feature is a 26-foot statue of Smokey Bear, a major mascot for the prevention of wildfires. You can see him and two small cubs next to him in the middle of the park.

Best Time to Visit: The park hosts many public events during the summer season. You can see the Smokey Bear statue decked out in various attire items and decorations throughout the year.

Pass/Permit/Fees: You can reach the park for free.

Closest City or Town:
International Falls

Physical Address:
214 6th Ave #2336, International Falls, MN 56649

GPS Coordinates:
48.60361 ° N, 93.40848 ° W

Did You Know? The park is also home to a museum dedicated to football legend Bronko Nagurski. He was born in nearby Rainy River and lived in International Falls until he died in 1990.

Voyageurs National Park

Voyageurs National Park is one of the country's northernmost national parks. The park has about 200,000 acres of land with many small lakes scattered around its area. You will find the Ellsworth Rock Gardens which feature abstract sculptures carved from rock surfaces. You can also travel to the far eastern end near the Canadian border to see Kettle Falls, a waterfall near Ontario's Kettle Island.

Best Time to Visit: The Northern Lights can be seen from the area at night. Look for an evening where the sky is clear, as it is easier to see the Northern Lights then. They are also more likely to occur in the winter.

Pass/Permit/Fees: You can visit the park for free, but it costs extra to hire a boat or canoe for water travel.

Closest City or Town:
International Falls

Physical Address:
Park Headquarters, 360 Hwy 11 East, International Falls, MN 56649

GPS Coordinates:
48.50643 ° N, 92.91178 ° W

Did You Know? The area has several useful sites for canoeing, as French-Canadian fur traders would often prepare routes for travel when bringing items out to the United States.

Long Lake

Located in the town of the same name in Hennepin County, Long Lake is a gentle oasis outside of the Twin Cities. Long Lake has a few curves and bends around the area to create a detailed scene with many trees lining the outside.

The lake has a beach on the southeastern end, plus it features a few boating spots. The Nelson Lakeside Park is a space for picnics, while the supper club to the south has a private dock where you can get a boat out to the water.

Best Time to Visit: The lake is easier to navigate during the summer months.

Pass/Permit/Fees: You can bring a boat to the lake for free, but you cannot rent one if you don't have a boat yourself.

Closest City or Town:
Long Lake

Physical Address:
Long Lake, MN 55356

GPS Coordinates:
44.98992 ° N, 93.55710 ° W

Did You Know? Long Lake is one of the smallest suburbs in the Minneapolis area. The town has a population of about 1,700 as of 2020.

Minneopa State Park

The Minneopa State Park is west of Mankato. It is famous for being home to a massive bison trail. The bison can appear around nearly 330 acres of land throughout the park. The park estimates there are at least twenty bison here, with at least one adult bull or male on hand to support conservation efforts. The park also includes a few views of the Minnesota River to the north. The Minneopa Creek to the west flows north to the river.

Best Time to Visit: The Bison Drive Road is open from Thursday to Tuesday each week but closed on Wednesdays for maintenance. You'll find many viewing spaces for the bison out here.

Pass/Permit/Fees: You can rent a GPS unit, birding kit, or various sports equipment from the visitor center. The cost varies per item, and not all items are guaranteed to be available.

Closest City or Town: Mankato

Physical Address:
54497 Gadwall Rd, Mankato, MN 56001

GPS Coordinates:
44.14719 ° N, 94.09173 ° W

Did You Know? Be sure to give the bison here at least 75 feet of clearance. They can be dangerous if their young calves are in the area.

American Swedish Institute

The American Swedish Institute celebrates the role of Swedish Americans and their influence in American history. The ASI in Minneapolis is partially housed in an early-twentieth-century mansion with a museum that showcases the history of Sweden and includes many artifacts from the country. The ASI also has a library and archive section that includes records on Scandinavian immigration to the United States in the nineteenth and twentieth centuries. FIKA, a Nordic-inspired café, is open from Thursday to Sunday for lunch and serves traditional Swedish meals.

Best Time to Visit:
The institute hosts a Christmas display every winter that shows how Christmas is celebrated in Sweden and other Northern European countries.

Pass/Permit/Fees:
Admission is $12 for adults and $6 for kids. An average meal at the café costs about $15.

Closest City or Town:
Minneapolis

Physical Address:
2600 Park Ave, Minneapolis, MN 55407

GPS Coordinates:
44.95465 ° N, 93.26581 ° W

Did You Know?
Nearly a quarter of a million Swedes immigrated to Minnesota from 1850 to 1930.

Bde Maka Ska (Lake Calhoun)

Bde Maka Ska, or Lake Calhoun as it was once called, is in the Chain of Lakes in Minneapolis. With a surface area of about 400 acres, it is the largest lake in the city. The lake houses Thomas Beach in the south and the 32nd Street Beach in the east. The lake is open for swimming, boating, and fishing. The place is also popular in the winter for ice fishing, as northern pikes and walleye are easy to find during the season. The Grand Rounds trail goes around the entire lake and features paths for biking and skating.

Best Time to Visit:
Conditions are most comfortable in the summer season.

Pass/Permit/Fees:
The lake is free to visit.

Closest City or Town:
Minneapolis

Physical Address:
3000 Calhoun Pkwy, Minneapolis, MN 55408

GPS Coordinates:
44.94372 ° N, 93.32123 ° W

Did You Know?
Bde Maka Ska is Dakota for "Lake White Earth." It was renamed Lake Calhoun in the nineteenth century after Secretary of War John Calhoun, but it was changed to its native name due to disputes over Calhoun's staunch support of slavery.

Cedar Lake

Cedar Lake is part of the Chain of Lakes in Minneapolis. It is west of the city and is directly west of Lake of the Isles. Cedar Lake features three swimming beaches and is also a popular site for fishing, with the bowfin, black bullhead, and green sunfish being among the most notable fish in the lake. You'll find a hiking trail on the south and western parts that leads to a local wetland area.

Best Time to Visit:
The summer is an easier time to visit, as conditions won't be freezing then. The longer days allow you to see downtown Minneapolis from the middle of the lake.

Pass/Permit/Fees:
You can visit the lake for free, but you will require a fishing license if you wish to fish here. The MN Department of Natural Resources can help you obtain your license.

Closest City or Town:
Minneapolis

Physical Address:
2101 Cedar Lake Parkway, Minneapolis, MN 55416

GPS Coordinates:
44.95999 ° N, 93.32101 ° W

Did You Know?
The Henry Neils House is on the eastern shore of the lake. The house is a Frank Lloyd Wright-designed property built in the 1950s.

Chain of Lakes Regional Park

You'll find the shorelines of many lakes at the Chain of Lakes Regional Park. The park has walking and hiking trails that lead to Brownie Lake, Lake Harriet, Bde Maka Ska, and Lake of the Isles. Many of these trails will lead you to Lyndale Park. Swimming beaches are open on Lake Harriet and Bde Maka Ska. There's also a dog park at Lake of the Isles. A bird sanctuary and small garden space are both in the Lyndale Park area.

Best Time to Visit:
You'll find some ice and hockey rinks around the park during the winter season.

Pass/Permit/Fees:
The park is free to visit. Canoe, boat, and bike rentals are available at the park.

Closest City or Town:
Minneapolis

Physical Address:
Water Works at Mill Ruins Park, 425 West River Parkway, Minneapolis, MN 55401

GPS Coordinates:
44.92641 ° N, 93.29710 ° W

Did You Know?
The trails take up about fifteen miles of space. Most of the trails are paved, making it easy for you to travel down them by bicycle.

Children's Theatre Company

The Children's Theatre Company is one of the most historic theaters in the Minneapolis area. The theater has been entertaining children with Theatre for Early Years programs since 1965 with various events throughout the year.

The theater is also popular for its theater arts classes for grade-school kids on dance, singing, improv, acting for the camera, and puppetry. The venue also has a virtual academy.

Best Time to Visit:
The theater has multiple shows during each season. Visit childrenstheatre.org for the latest details on what shows are coming to the venue.

Pass/Permit/Fees:
Prices for shows will vary by event.

Closest City or Town:
Minneapolis

Physical Address:
2400 3rd Ave S, Minneapolis, MN 55404

GPS Coordinates:
44.95857 ° N, 93.27335 ° W

Did You Know?
The theater focuses on a mix of classic and contemporary shows for kids. Most of its shows are open for kids of all ages, although some are more suitable for kids eight or older.

Guthrie Theater

The Guthrie Theater is a popular performing arts theater in Minneapolis. The theater hosts many plays and musicals throughout the year, including some Shakespeare productions. There are also holiday-themed events here during the winter season. The theater features three separate stages, plus it has a cantilevered bridge that links between sites. The outside of the theater is noteworthy for having a modern design.

Best Time to Visit:
Showtimes at the Guthrie Theater change with each season. Visit the theater website for a current program schedule

Pass/Permit/Fees:
Ticket prices will vary by show.

Closest City or Town:
Minneapolis

Physical Address:
818 S 2nd St, Minneapolis, MN 55415

GPS Coordinates:
44.97820 ° N, 93.25584 ° W

Did You Know?
The current building that houses the Guthrie Theater opened in 2006. The theater has been in operation since 1963.

Lake Harriet

Lake Harriet is in southwest Minneapolis and is part of the Chain of Lakes. The lake is 335 acres in surface area and is popular for sailing and other water activities, plus it is open for fishing.

You will find two beaches at Lake Harriet, with one being to the north and the other in the south. You can also visit Beard's Plaisance in the southwest and enjoy play time with the family. The area has a few public tennis courts and room for picnics.

Best Time to Visit:
The spring and summer seasons are the most active times at the Thomas Sadler Roberts Bird Sanctuary, which is on the northern end of Lake Harriet.

Pass/Permit/Fees:
There is no admission for visiting Lake Harriet.

Closest City or Town:
Minneapolis

Physical Address:
4135 W Lake Harriet Pkwy, Minneapolis, MN 55409

GPS Coordinates:
44.92101 ° N, 93.30465 ° W

Did You Know?
The Lakewood Cemetery is to the north of Lake Harriet. The cemetery has a chapel inspired by Istanbul's Hagia Sophia. The cemetery is also the final resting site of Hubert Humphrey and his wife.

Lake Hiawatha

You will find Lake Hiawatha in southern Minneapolis near the MSP Airport. The lake has about 50 acres of room for fishing, plus there are some wading areas in the eastern end.

The lake has a public beach to the east, while the northeastern end has a few tennis courts and softball fields. There's also a golf course to the west. You'll find multiple cycling paths that circle the entire area of the lake on the outside.

Best Time to Visit:
Most of the spaces around Lake Hiawatha are open during the summer.

Pass/Permit/Fees:
It will cost extra to go golfing at the course here or to rent a bicycle from the bike park to the south. The price will vary by season.

Closest City or Town:
Minneapolis

Physical Address:
2701 E 44th St, Minneapolis, MN 55406

GPS Coordinates:
44.92095 ° N, 93.23646 ° W

Did You Know?
Minnehaha Creek flows through the southern end of Lake Hiawatha. The creek moves towards the Mississippi River to the east.

Lake of the Isles

Lake of the Isles is in the northern part of the Chain of Lakes in Minneapolis. The lake is about 110 acres in area and includes a park area to the south. There's a walking and cycling trail that goes across the entire body of the lake and two small islands in the middle. Raspberry Island and Mike's Island are uninhabited masses with many trees throughout their areas. The islands are accessible by boat from a dock in the south or a canoe launch to the north, but there are no docks on the islands themselves.

Best Time to Visit:
The lake is popular during the winter season as a spot for ice skating and pond hockey.

Pass/Permit/Fees:
You can visit for free, but the cost to rent a vessel for paddling will vary by provider.

Closest City or Town:
Minneapolis

Physical Address:
2500 Lake of the Isles Parkway E, Minneapolis, MN 55405

GPS Coordinates:
44.95529 ° N, 93.30836 ° W

Did You Know?
There were originally four islands at Lake of the Isles, but two islands to the south were converted into park space.

Lake Nokomis Beach

Lake Nokomis in Minneapolis is a peaceful lake open for swimming on the northwestern part of the lake. Lake Nokomis Beach is a public beach run by the state's parks board.

You can relax on the water, or you can rent a paddleboat to the north. A boat launch for private boats is to the south. There's also a cycling trail that goes through the beach and circles the entire lake. You can rent a bicycle to go down the trail if you wish.

Best Time to Visit:
Most of the features here are open in the summer.

Pass/Permit/Fees:
While admission to the beach is free, it will cost extra to rent a bicycle or anything else. You may also require a reservation if you want to use the boat launch.

Closest City or Town:
Minneapolis

Physical Address:
4955 W Lake Nokomis Parkway, Minneapolis, MN 55417

GPS Coordinates:
44.91175 ° N, 93.24228 ° W

Did You Know?
Lake Nokomis is named after the grandmother of Hiawatha.

Mill City Museum

The flour industry is the focus of the Mill City Museum in Minneapolis. The museum is part of a mill complex from the 1870s. The facility features a flour milling site and includes a variety of nineteenth-century milling equipment. You will also see millstones and other items utilized in the production of flour.

Much of the museum houses the ruins of an old mill built in the late nineteenth century. The old turbine pits and engine houses used for helping facilitate flour production are still intact.

Best Time to Visit:
The museum's courtyard hosts a farmers' market on Saturdays from May to September. The market is also on select Saturdays during the offseason

Pass/Permit/Fees:
Admission is $12 for adults and $6 for kids.

Closest City or Town:
Minneapolis

Physical Address:
704 S 2nd St, Minneapolis, MN 55401

GPS Coordinates:
44.97884 ° N, 93.25744 ° W

Did You Know?
You'll notice the Gold Medal Flour sign at the top of the museum building. The flour brand was introduced and first produced in Minneapolis.

Minneapolis Institute of Art

The Minneapolis Institute of Art houses art pieces spreading over 5,000 years. You will find art from all corners of the world, including some pieces of Native American work.

The museum has separate wings devoted to European, African, and Asian art. You'll also see many pieces of Chinese architecture and jade materials here. The museum has about 90,000 items in its collection.

Best Time to Visit:
The MIA hosts various exhibitions showcasing different aspects of art. Past exhibitions have focused on things like Japanese calligraphy, Imperial China works, and art from India. Visit new.artsmia.org to see what exhibitions are on display before your visit.

Pass/Permit/Fees:
General admission is free, but it may cost extra to visit one of the special exhibitions here.

Closest City or Town:
Minneapolis

Physical Address:
2400 3rd Ave S, Minneapolis, MN 55404

GPS Coordinates:
44.95856 ° N, 93.27314 ° W

Did You Know?
Some of the artists whose work is on display here include Henri Matisse, Rembrandt, and El Greco.

Minneapolis Sculpture Garden

The Minneapolis Sculpture Garden has eleven acres of outdoor land near the Walker Art Center. The garden features many unique outdoor pieces of art, including some shadow imprints on the walkways and many creative pieces with interpretive shapes.

Spoonbridge and Cherry is the most iconic sculpture you'll find here. The 1988 sculpture has a massive, curved spoon with a cherry on the end. A small pond surrounds the area. The structure is a symbol of the city of Minneapolis.

Best Time to Visit:
The garden is open until midnight every day. Some of the sculptures here will stand out well at night, especially as the Minneapolis skyline appears in the background in some spots.

Pass/Permit/Fees:
You can visit the garden for free.

Closest City or Town:
Minneapolis

Physical Address:
725 Vineland Pl, Minneapolis, MN 55403

GPS Coordinates:
44.97023 ° N, 93.28890 ° W

Did You Know?
You can walk directly from Loring Park to the sculpture garden. There's a small pedestrian bridge between the two.

Minnehaha Falls

The city of Minneapolis has its own unique waterfall at Minnehaha Falls. The waterfall is part of Minnehaha Creek, a body of water that moves towards the Mississippi River to the east. Minnehaha Falls is less than a mile from the river. The waterfall has a gentle flow, although it is more intense following rainfall. You can reach the waterfall through various cycling and walking trails around the park. The waterfall is inside the Minnehaha Regional Park and is to the east of the Hiawatha statue.

Best Time to Visit:
The waterfall produces a distinct frozen body during the winter season. You can walk behind the frozen waterfall during the winter, although you will require proper winter protection before doing so.

Pass/Permit/Fees:
You can visit the area for free. You can also rent a bicycle or other equipment at the visitor's center here, but the cost for doing so will vary.

Closest City or Town:
Minneapolis

Physical Address:
4801 S Minnehaha Dr, Minneapolis, MN 55417

GPS Coordinates:
44.91535 ° N, 93.21100 ° W

Did You Know?
The bottom part of the creek is the lowest surface point in Minneapolis. It is about 700 feet above sea level.

Minnehaha Regional Park

The Minnehaha Regional Park is a fun recreational area in Minneapolis off of the Mississippi River. The park houses the end of the Minnehaha Creek as it leads into the river. You'll find a small waterfall in the middle part of the creek. The 170-acre park houses statues of the Iroquois Confederacy leader Hiawatha and Swedish poet Gunnar Wennerberg. The park also has a late-nineteenth-century train depot and a mansion once owned by local businessman Robert F. Jones. There are also a few gardens around the park. Some of the gardens include skunk cabbage, a spring-blooming plant with a circular look.

Best Time to Visit:
The park is most beautiful in the winter, especially as the waterfall freezes.

Pass/Permit/Fees:
Admission is free, but it will cost extra to rent a bicycle.

Closest City or Town:
Minneapolis

Physical Address:
4801 S Minnehaha Dr, Minneapolis, MN 55417

GPS Coordinates:
44.91547 ° N, 93.21092 ° W

Did You Know?
One of Minneapolis's unofficial symbols is a tree in the middle of this park that has been "decorated" with several wads of chewing gum. The tree is cleaned on occasion, but people still place their chewed gum on the trunk.

Nicollet Mall

Nicollet Mall is a twelve-block shopping and dining district in downtown Minneapolis. The mall houses the flagship Target department store near Target's global headquarters.

The Walker Art Center is in Nicollet Mall, and the Minnesota Orchestra's concert hall is also here. The Minneapolis Central Library is located at the northern end of the mall. The Mary Tyler Moore statue on 7th Avenue is the most popular attraction of Nicollet Mall. The statue pays tribute to her eponymous television show, which was set in Minneapolis.

Best Time to Visit:
Nicollet Mall hosts the Holidazzle Village in the winter months. The village is part of a vast Christmas celebration, which includes an annual parade.

Pass/Permit/Fees:
It is free to go around Nicollet Mall.

Closest City or Town:
Minneapolis

Physical Address:
555 Nicollet Mall, Minneapolis, MN 55403

GPS Coordinates:
44.97864 ° N, 93.27093 ° W

Did You Know?
The Nicollet Skyway features about eight miles of elevated and enclosed pedestrian bridges. It covers eighty city blocks.

Snelling Lake Trail, Fort Snelling State Park

The Snelling Lake Trail is in the western part of Fort Snelling State Park. The trail has a paved surface for biking and hiking. It starts in the south near the end of the Fort Snelling National Cemetery and goes east of the Minnesota River. The trail moves north to the southern part of the historic Fort Snelling property.

The northern part of the trail connects to the Minnehaha Trail which goes north to the Minnehaha Regional Park.

Best Time to Visit:
The trail is easier to move through in the daytime, as most of the trail isn't illuminated.

Pass/Permit/Fees:
The trail is free to visit.

Closest City or Town:
Minneapolis

Physical Address:
101 Snelling Lake Rd, St. Paul, MN 55111

GPS Coordinates:
44.87397 ° N, 93.19165 ° W

Did You Know?
The trail is not far from the Fort Snelling National Cemetery, where many military members from the state are buried.

Target Field

Target Field is the home of the Minnesota Twins baseball team in downtown Minneapolis. The team has played at the ballpark since 2010. The ballpark's name is sponsored by the Target department store, a company based in Minneapolis. It has a roof deck in the left-field area that also includes a bonfire. The place also has a few restaurants, including some concession stands that sell foods you may find at the Minnesota State Fair. The park also has statues of many former Twins players. You will find statues of Harmon Killebrew, Rod Carew, Kirby Puckett, and former owner Carl Pohlad.

Best Time to Visit:
Tours are open throughout the baseball season. Check with the Twins first to see when tours are open.

Pass/Permit/Fees:
Tours are $18 for adults and $13 for kids.

Closest City or Town:
Minneapolis

Physical Address:
600 N 1st Ave, Minneapolis, MN 55403

GPS Coordinates:
44.98173 ° N, 93.27758 ° W

Did You Know?
The outfield area has a massive display featuring Minnie and Paul, the team's original mascots.

U.S. Bank Stadium

U.S. Bank Stadium in Minneapolis is the home of the Minnesota Vikings football team. The University of Minnesota Golden Gophers baseball team also plays here. The stadium opened in 2016 on the footprint of the Metrodome, the Vikings' former home stadium. It features a fixed roof with a design inspired by Nordic vernacular architecture. The roof design allows it to handle massive amounts of snow. The layout also includes a glass panel that lets people see downtown Minneapolis from inside the building. The venue is a popular site for major sporting events. It has hosted the Super Bowl and the NCAA Final Four.

Best Time to Visit:
Tours are available throughout the year.

Pass/Permit/Fees:
Ticket prices for tours will vary throughout the year.

Closest City or Town:
Minneapolis

Physical Address:
401 Chicago Ave, Minneapolis, MN 55415

GPS Coordinates:
44.97381 ° N, 93.25702 ° W

Did You Know?
Inline roller-skating activities are often held inside the stadium, although the hours for skating will vary throughout the year.

Walker Art Center

The Walker Art Center in Minneapolis is an art museum that focuses on contemporary art from 1960 to the present. The museum has thousands of art pieces from artists like Edward Hopper, Andy Warhol, Chuck Close, and Yves Klein. It also features a moving image center that houses films from Marcel Duchamp and Salvador Dali.

The center houses various art installations in its outdoor space. One of the more unique features is an interactive miniature golf course with holes inspired by many artistic concepts featured at the museum.

Best Time to Visit:
The museum has many exhibitions that change during the year. Visit walkerart.org to learn about what is showing here at any time.

Pass/Permit/Fees:
Admission is $15 for adults and $5 for kids.

Closest City or Town:
Minneapolis

Physical Address:
725 Vineland Pl, Minneapolis, MN 55403

GPS Coordinates:
44.96820 ° N, 93.28862 ° W

Did You Know?
The center is part of a complex that links with the Minneapolis Sculpture Garden.

Weisman Art Museum

You will notice a distinct look to the Weisman Art Museum on the University of Minnesota campus in Minneapolis. The Frank Gehry-designed building features a stainless-steel look that has the appearance of several small skyscrapers coming from the body.

The museum has a collection of more than 20,000 items. The venue features entertaining abstract pieces produced in many forms.

Best Time to Visit:
Visit during the summer, when you will find many new art productions from U of M students.

Pass/Permit/Fees:
Admission to the museum is free.

Closest City or Town:
Minneapolis

Physical Address:
333 E River Pkwy, Minneapolis, MN 55455

GPS Coordinates:
44.97317 ° N, 93.23731 ° W

Did You Know?
Gehry's design for the outside includes many skylights that appear at varying places around the museum. Some of the paintings are arranged based on how sensitive they are to the light that comes in.

Hjemkomst Viking Ship

The Hjemkomst Center in Moorhead is a museum that explores the Norwegian influence on Minnesota's history. The center has a replica of the Hopperstad Stave Church, a Catholic church building in Norway.

The most popular part of the center is the Hjemkomst Viking Ship, a replica of an eighth-century burial ship. The ship is nearly forty feet long and features a 45-foot mast. The wooden body is arched and designed to show what was used and eventually set on fire when burying Vikings. The ship was built in the 1970s and sailed to Bergen and Oslo before returning to Minnesota.

Best Time to Visit:
The Viking ship is indoors, so you can visit any time.

Pass/Permit/Fees:
The surrounding museum costs $7 for adults to visit or $5 for kids.

Closest City or Town:
Moorhead

Physical Address:
202 1st Ave N, Moorhead, MN 56560

GPS Coordinates:
46.87791 ° N, 96.77858 ° W

Did You Know? Hjemkomst is a Norwegian word for "homecoming."

Sibley State Park

Sibley State Park is north of Andrew Lake in Kandiyohi County. The park has a campground on the northern shore of the lake. You will find a few camping sites around the area here.

The park has a few stone buildings dating to the 1930s and features many forms of wildlife like white-tailed deer and gray foxes. The site is also popular for birdwatching, as you will find ruffled grouses, Canada geese, and scarlet tanagers around the park.

Best Time to Visit:
The summer is a wonderful time to visit, as the water conditions in the beach area to the south are more comfortable.

Pass/Permit/Fees:
Admission to the park is free.

Closest City or Town:
New London

Physical Address:
800 Sibley Park Rd NE, New London, MN 56273

GPS Coordinates:
45.32283 ° N, 95.04668

Did You Know?
The park takes its name from Henry Sibley, the state's first governor.

Itasca State Park

The furthest northern parts of the Mississippi River appear in the Itasca State Park. The park includes Lake Itasca, a spot considered to be the main source of the river.

The areas around Lake Itasca are mostly undisturbed, including red pine trees that are several centuries old. You can go down the western arm of the lake to see where the Mississippi River begins, creating a body of water that flows down south to New Orleans.

Best Time to Visit:
Local conditions are comfortable during the summer season. The temperatures rarely go over 30 degrees in the winter.

Pass/Permit/Fees:
You can visit the park for free. You can also stay at one of the cabins around the park, although they are mostly in the southeastern and northern parts.

Closest City or Town:
Park Rapids

Physical Address:
36750 Main Park Dr, Park Rapids, MN 56470

GPS Coordinates:
47.18881 ° N, 95.14974 ° W

Did You Know?
You'll find more than a hundred bird species throughout the park. Bald eagles are known to migrate through the area during the fall season.

Pipestone National Monument

The Pipestone National Monument is in the southwestern end of Minnesota. The monument is home to quarries that were used by many people in the Dakota, Lakota, and Sioux tribes. The area was neutral territory for natives, as the catlinite stone here could be quarried for the production of ceremonial pipes. You will find an Indian shrine at the monument, plus you can hike the Circle Trail to the Nicollet Expedition Marker. The marker shows where Joseph Nicollet traveled when mapping the Mississippi River in the 1830s.

Best Time to Visit:
The venue hosts many indoor events throughout the year, including cultural demonstrations of different pipe-producing activities. The calendar of events will change during the year.

Pass/Permit/Fees:
Admission is free.

Closest City or Town:
Pipestone

Physical Address:
36 Reservation Ave, Pipestone, MN 56164

GPS Coordinates:
44.01393 ° N, 96.32441 ° W

Did You Know?
Bison have been found around the monument, although they are more prominent about twenty miles south at the Blue Mounds State Park.

Cascade Meadow Wetlands & Environmental Science Center

The Saint Mary's University of Minnesota operates the Cascade Meadow Wetlands and Environmental Science Center in Rochester. The center has exhibits on energy, water, and sustainable operations. You'll also find four separate trails that go throughout the wetlands. The trails include ones that go by many unique operations including wind energy turbines and another that explores how rainwater can be reused for many purposes.

Best Time to Visit:
The trails are open from sunrise to sunset each day.

Pass/Permit/Fees:
While you can visit for free, you cannot bring your dog here for walking. Dog waste could potentially harm the local creek waters.

Closest City or Town:
Rochester

Physical Address:
2900 19th St NW, Rochester, MN 55901

GPS Coordinates:
44.03951 ° N, 92.50548 ° W

Did You Know?
Seven of the eight types of wetlands in the state of Minnesota are represented at the center. You'll also find three types of prairies.

Heritage House Victorian Museum

Take a visit to the Victorian era at the Heritage House in Rochester. The 1875 house is an Italianate building that houses many Victorian-era artifacts, including of furniture, outfits, and other items. The house explores the lives of people in Minnesota during the late nineteenth century.

The Heritage House has been refurbished to its original 1875 structure. The building survived an 1883 tornado that destroyed much of the rest of the city, making it one of Rochester's oldest buildings.

Best Time to Visit:
Tours are available from June to August.

Pass/Permit/Fees:
Admission on a tour is $5 for adults and $3 for kids. The house is not handicap-accessible.

Closest City or Town:
Rochester

Physical Address:
Central Park, 225 1st Ave NW, Rochester, MN 55901

GPS Coordinates:
44.02612 ° N, 92.46478 ° W

Did You Know?
The Heritage House's current location in the Central Park area of Rochester is not its original site. The property was relocated to the area in 1972.

History Center of Olmsted County

The History Center of Olmsted County is on more than fifty acres of land. The center has two farmsteads with a few old buildings on those properties.

The center features exhibits surrounding the history of Rochester and southern Minnesota. These include exhibits on military service, how the nearby Mayo Clinic has helped advance healthcare, and how farming activities worked in the area across generations.

Best Time to Visit:
The History Center has a regular schedule of events. Visit olmstedhistory.com to learn more about some of the events here and what is happening before your visit.

Pass/Permit/Fees:
Admission is $5 for adults and $2 for kids.

Closest City or Town:
Rochester

Physical Address:
1195 W Circle Dr SW, Rochester, MN 55902

GPS Coordinates:
44.00630 ° N, 92.50946 ° W

Did You Know?
The center has a community garden that operates during the spring and summer seasons. Patrons can donate $75 for an annual plot where they can prepare various plants or vegetables.

Mayowood Mansion

The Mayowood Mansion in Rochester is a 38-room mansion built in 1911 for Dr. Charlie Mayo, the co-founder of the nearby Mayo Clinic. You can tour the inside of the mansion and see many artifacts illustrating Mayo's work and highlighting how he and the other doctors at the Mayo Clinic have helped revolutionize medicine.

The mansion also has a garden space on the outside and an East Asian tea house on the property grounds. The eastern end of the grounds features an old stone barn.

Best Time to Visit:
Tours mostly occur on the weekends here. The place is also decorated in November and December for the Christmas season.

Pass/Permit/Fees:
Admission is $17 for adults and $5 for kids.

Closest City or Town:
Rochester

Physical Address:
3720 Mayowood Rd SW, Rochester, MN 55902

GPS Coordinates:
43.99116 ° N, 92.52131 ° W

Did You Know?
Part of the mansion is built on a private lake that was included in the Mayo family's mansion grounds. The lake has been named Mayowood Lake in the property's honor.

Plummer House of the Arts

The Plummer House in Rochester is a Tudor Revival house built in 1924. The house was the home of Dr. Henry Plummer, one of the founders of the Mayo Clinic.

The house has 49 rooms and holds five stories of space. It is open for tours, and many arts events. These include concerts, art galleries, and drama performances. The events are part of the Plummer family's desire to create an open environment for everyone to enjoy life.

Best Time to Visit:
Tours are held on Wednesdays in the summer.

Pass/Permit/Fees:
Tours are $10 for adults and $5 for kids.

Closest City or Town:
Rochester

Physical Address:
1091 Plummer Ln SW, Rochester, MN 55902

GPS Coordinates:
44.01059 ° N, 92.47942 ° W

Did You Know?
The Plummer House was the first house in Rochester to have a gas furnace. Other innovative features in the house included a security system, an intercom system, and a dumbwaiter.

Quarry Hill Nature Center

The Quarry Hill Nature Center in Rochester is a park space with several hiking trails. You can walk by the Prairie House to the east, or you can see the Silver Creek in the western and southern parts of the park. The nature center has more than thirty live animals and birds on display. You can see many turtles, snakes, and tree frogs here. There's also an indoor honeybee hive and a bird study room at the center as well as some hands-on attractions where you can explore some of the more intricate parts of nature. From the patterns on a turtle's shell to how moose antlers are formed and shaped, you will learn many things about the animals that live in Minnesota.

Best Time to Visit:
The nature center is open on weekends. The park and trail spaces are open every day.

Pass/Permit/Fees:
Admission is free, although donations are encouraged.

Closest City or Town:
Rochester

Physical Address:
701 Silver Creek Rd NE, Rochester, MN 55906

GPS Coordinates:
44.03019 ° N, 92.43026 ° W

Did You Know?
The nature center is the home to a fifty-year-old snapping turtle named Fredricka. She is considered the mascot of the center.

Rochester Art Center

The Rochester Art Center is a gallery highlighting art from around the world. It hosts many exhibits, including some seasonal events presenting art from many cultures.

The center also has an art gallery with an open studio for adults and teens. People can sign up to participate in various art activities while at the center, making it one of the most interactive places to visit in Rochester.

Best Time to Visit:
The art center hosts many programs throughout the year. The schedule always changes, so visit the center's website at rochesterartcenter.org to see what is there.

Pass/Permit/Fees:
Admission is $5 for adults.

Closest City or Town:
Rochester

Physical Address:
30 Civic Center Dr SE, STE 120, Rochester, MN 55904

GPS Coordinates:
44.02145 ° N, 92.45844 ° W

Did You Know?
The art center has been in operation since 1946, but its current location was built in 2004.

The Plummer Building

The Plummer Building was built in 1928 in downtown Rochester and is located on the Mayo Clinic campus.

The building has many bas-reliefs designs reflective of the Mayo family's English heritage. The top has a 56-bell carillon that overlooks the city and produces music.

The third floor houses the offices of Drs. Charlie and Will Mayo. It includes many artifacts surrounding their work in medicine, including their 1950 Nobel Prize.

Best Time to Visit:
The building is open year-round.

Pass/Permit/Fees:
The Historical Suite is open for tours. It is free to the public.

Closest City or Town:
Rochester

Physical Address:
100 2nd St SW, Rochester, MN 55902

GPS Coordinates:
44.02200 ° N, 92.46543 ° W

Did You Know?
The building has two 4,000-pound bronze doors at the entrance. The doors are almost always kept open, a symbol of the clinic's willingness to accept people who need medical support.

Robinson's Ice Cave

Go to the southern end of Banning State Park in Pine County to reach Robinson's Ice Cave. The cave is 200 feet deep and is home to various bat species that hibernate in the area.

You will not be able to enter the cave, as the cave has a gate to ensure the bats inside stay safe and undisturbed. You will find various waterfalls around the area, with some of them freezing over during the winter season.

Best Time to Visit:
The cave area looks its best in the winter, as icicles and frozen waterfalls add a unique touch.

Pass/Permit/Fees:
The area is free to enter.

Closest City or Town:
Sandstone

Physical Address:
Quarry Parking, 1602 MN-23, Sandstone, MN 55072

GPS Coordinates:
46.14262 ° N, 92.86203 ° W

Did You Know?
You will find many birch and aspen trees, although some Norwegian pines will appear at the ends of the park leading to the cave.

Valleyfair

Valleyfair is an amusement park in Shakopee that has been entertaining people in the Twin Cities since 1976. Valleyfair has amusement rides for the family including nine roller coasters. You can take a drop of nearly 200 feet on the Wild Thing, or you can go through three loops on the Corkscrew coaster. The High Roller coaster has been open since 1976 and still goes 50 miles per hour. You'll also find the Soak City waterpark in Valleyfair. The Planet Snoopy area offers many fun activities for kids.

Best Time to Visit:
Valleyfair is open from May to October, but it is only open on weekends during the early and late parts of the season.

Pass/Permit/Fees:
Daily tickets are available for as little as $35 per person.

Closest City or Town:
Shakopee

Physical Address:
1 Valley Fair Dr, Shakopee, MN 55379

GPS Coordinates:
44.79970 ° N, 93.45574 ° W

Did You Know?
Valleyfair is part of the Cedar Fair group of theme parks. The group that owns the Cedar Point theme park in Ohio acquired Valleyfair in 1978 to form the Cedar Fair company.

Temperance River

The Temperance River is about forty miles long and starts at Brule Lake in the Temperance River State Park. The river flows toward Lake Superior, eventually emptying between the Upper and Lower Campgrounds.

The park has many narrow spaces for wading, but it also has a few deep spots for fishing. You can take the Superior Hiking Trail on either side of the river.

Best Time to Visit:
The spring is an ideal time, as conditions will be a little easier for travel. Be sure you bring the proper footwear here.

Pass/Permit/Fees:
The river is free to travel around.

Closest City or Town:
Schroeder

Physical Address:
7620 West Hwy 61, Schroeder, MN 55613

GPS Coordinates:
47.55479 ° N, 90.87387 ° W

Did You Know?
Unlike most other rivers leading to Lake Superior, the Temperance River does not have a sand bar near its mouth.

Forestville/Mystery Cave State Park

Forestville is a ghost town in Fillmore County in the southeastern part of the state. The town was formed in the 1850s, but it struggled due to a lack of railroad access. The town was abandoned in 1910, but you can find some of the remnants of the old buildings in the area. You'll also come across the Mystery Cave State Park while in Forestville. The cave features about thirteen miles of underground trails. You can tour many of the cave trails and see some of the formations and pools inside the area.

Best Time to Visit:
The park is in season during the spring, summer, and fall months. The caves are 48 degrees Fahrenheit throughout the year, so be sure to dress accordingly if you wish to visit the cave.

Pass/Permit/Fees:
Tours of the cave area are $15 for adults and $10 for kids.

Closest City or Town:
Spring Valley

Physical Address:
21071 County Rd 118, Preston, MN 55965

GPS Coordinates:
43.64068 ° N, 92.21709 ° W

Did You Know?
Various flowstones, fossils, and stalactites can be found throughout the inside of the cave. But the area is off-limits for carving and harvesting, as some spots around the cave may be too fragile for exploration.

Munsinger Clemens Gardens

Munsinger Clemens Gardens is on the Mississippi River in St. Cloud. The gardens have tall pine trees lining many spaces including a few greenhouses. You will find rose vines, an arbor trellis, and a perennial garden. The rose garden here features more than a thousand roses in many forms. A lily pond and a rock garden are also inside the land.

The gardens also feature a few fountains. The perennial garden has a cast-iron fountain based on a pre-Civil War fountain in Georgia. These and other sites around the garden are accessible off a trail leading from the eastern shore of the river.

Best Time to Visit:
The gardens are open from the spring to the fall.

Pass/Permit/Fees:
There are no admission fees.

Closest City or Town:
St. Cloud

Physical Address:
1515 Riverside Dr SE, St. Cloud, MN 56304

GPS Coordinates:
45.55152 ° N, 94.14441 ° W

Did You Know?
Part of the gardens here take their inspiration from the Sissinghurst Castle Garden in the United Kingdom.

Aamodt's Apple Orchard

The apples at Aamodt's Apple Orchard are in full harvest in the summer, fall, and winter. The orchard in Stillwater hosts several acres of farmland for apples. You'll find such apples as the State Fair, Beacon, Jonathan, Gala, McIntosh, Regent, Fireside, and Keepsake. The orchard houses an apple barn and bakery, plus there's a goat farm for kids. The orchard is also home to the Saint Croix Vineyards, one of the state's most popular wineries. You can order Thor's Hard Cider at the farm.

Best Time to Visit:
The orchard hosts most of its activities during the fall season. These include events where you can pick your own apples.

Pass/Permit/Fees:
While you can visit the orchard for free, it may cost extra to participate in some activities, including apple picking. Check with the orchard for details.

Closest City or Town:
Stillwater

Physical Address:
6428 Manning Ave N, Stillwater, MN 55082

GPS Coordinates:
45.04252 ° N, 92.86562 ° W

Did You Know?
Aamodt's Apple Orchard has been family-owned since Thor and Lucille Aamodt founded the place in 1948.

Brown's Creek Trail

The Brown's Creek Trail is a 5.9-mile trail from the town of Grant to Stillwater on the St. Croix River and the boundary with Wisconsin. The trail is on an old railroad grade. Part of the trail is surrounded by a broadleaf forest near Brown's Creek, a trout stream. The eastern end runs parallel to the St. Croix River, where you can see the National Scenic Riverway. The trail is open for hiking, biking, and skating.

Best Time to Visit:
You can visit during the winter, but the trail is not groomed for winter use.

Pass/Permit/Fees:
You can visit for free, but you'll require a horse pass for horseback riding. The Department of Natural Resources can provide you with a daily horse pass for $5, or a one-year pass for $21. The one-year pass is effective for that calendar year only.

Closest City or Town:
Stillwater

Physical Address:
575 Main St N, Stillwater, MN 55082

GPS Coordinates:
Stillwater: 45.05681 ° N, 92.80726 ° W
Grant: 45.08415 ° N, 92.91034 ° W

Did You Know?
Part of the trail goes through the Oak Glen Golf Course in Stillwater.

Lift Bridge Brewing Company

The state of Minnesota hosts an extensive microbrewing community. The Lift Bridge Brewing Company is one microbrewery that stands out in the state. You can visit the brewery in Stillwater to try some of the various beers made on site.

The brewery has a taproom where you can enjoy Lift Bridge beers of all sorts. You can also enjoy a brewery tour while out here. The place serves nonalcoholic products as well, including root beer, cream soda, or black cherry soda.

Best Time to Visit:
The brewery is open year-round.

Pass/Permit/Fees:
You can visit the area for free, although the prices for beers will vary. You can request a growler that you can fill with whatever beer you wish.

Closest City or Town:
Stillwater

Physical Address:
1900 Tower Dr W, Stillwater, MN 55082

GPS Coordinates:
45.03934 ° N, 92.83168 ° W

Did You Know?
Minnesota has more than 180 breweries throughout the state.

Saint Croix Vineyards

You will find many vineyards throughout Minnesota, including Saint Croix Vineyards in Stillwater. The vineyards have been in operation for nearly thirty years. Saint Croix houses a tasting room inside a century-old barn. You can enjoy red, white, and dessert wines while out here. Many of these wines have won awards for being among the best produced in cold climate areas.

Best Time to Visit:
The vineyards host various events during the summer, including live music events and painting parties. The venue hosts the annual Grape Stomp in September. People can compete to see who the most creative or entertaining grape stomper is.

Pass/Permit/Fees:
The vineyards offer free public tours on weekends. It costs $9 and up for a wine flight. You can also order wine bottles.

Closest City or Town:
Stillwater

Physical Address:
6428 Manning Ave N, Stillwater, MN 55082

GPS Coordinates:
45.04223 ° N, 92.86547 ° W

Did You Know?
Minnesota currently has more than forty wineries operating throughout the state. The total is a dramatic increase from the 1990s when there were only three wineries.

Stillwater Lift Bridge

The Stillwater Lift Bridge opened in 1931 and remains the last vertical-lift bridge to have been built in the state. The bridge is not open for vehicular use, but it is open for pedestrians and cyclists. It goes across the St. Croix River from downtown Stillwater to the St. Croix Loop trail in Houlton, Wisconsin. The bridge has been preserved to its original appearance. You can cross the bridge while continuing into a hiking trail in Wisconsin. You can also notice the original mechanisms used to help lift the middle part of the bridge for when boats go by.

Best Time to Visit:
The bridge is operational at times when boats need to go across. But the timeframe for when the bridge will lift up and down will vary throughout the year. There is no set schedule for when it is operational.

Pass/Permit/Fees:
The bridge is free to visit and cross.

Closest City or Town:
Stillwater

Physical Address:
106 Chestnut St E, Stillwater, MN 55082

GPS Coordinates:
45.05631 ° N, 92.80367 ° W

Did You Know?
The bridge had been open for vehicular use until 2017 when the opening of the St. Croix Crossing to the south opened.

Teddy Bear Park

Teddy Bear Park is a charming outdoor park in Stillwater. The park features a play area for young children, plus it has a small outdoor theater that hosts many kids' events each year. There's also a small barn with party rooms that people can reserve for special occasions.

Teddy Bear Park is named for the many teddy bear statues you'll find throughout the space. These include a few that kids can sit on and get their pictures taken.

Best Time to Visit:
Teddy Bear Park is open from April to October.

Pass/Permit/Fees:
Admission is free, plus there's a free parking lot next to the park.

Closest City or Town:
Stillwater

Physical Address:
207 Nelson St E, Stillwater, MN 55082

GPS Coordinates:
45.05371 ° N, 92.80594 ° W

Did You Know?
Most of the park features a farm theme. The theme carries over to the indoor meeting and party space.

Warden's House Museum

The Warden's House Museum in Stillwater is an 1853 home that was the official residence for the Minnesota Territorial Prison's warden until 1914. The two-story building features a limestone body with a Greek influence.

The house is among the few buildings remaining from the original prison. The building features period furniture and many artifacts from when the prison was in operation. Some of these items include things that once belonged to members of the James-Younger Gang.

Best Time to Visit:
The museum is open for tours from May to October.

Pass/Permit/Fees:
Admission is $5 for adults and $1 for kids.

Closest City or Town:
Stillwater

Physical Address:
602 Main St N, Stillwater, MN 55082

GPS Coordinates:
45.06172 ° N, 92.80759 ° W

Did You Know?
Most of the old prison was demolished in 1914 after the state moved its main prison to Bayport, where it still operates today.

Alexander Ramsey House

The Alexander Ramsey House in St. Paul is a Victorian house that was home to Alexander Ramsey, the state's first governor. The 1868 property includes many Victorian accents, including crystal chandeliers and marble fireplaces. The building also houses luxurious furniture pieces shipped from New York's A.T. Stewart Company Store. The Minnesota Historical Society has been in charge of the house since the death of the last Ramsey family member in 1964. The house is decorated to look as it did during the family's time in the house in the 1870s.

Best Time to Visit:
The house hosts a Christmas program every winter where the home is decorated for the holidays in a way the Ramsey family would have done. Many of the ornaments on the Christmas tree here were owned by the Ramsey family.

Pass/Permit/Fees:
Admission is $10 for adults.

Closest City or Town:
St. Paul

Physical Address:
265 Exchange St S, St. Paul, MN 55102

GPS Coordinates:
44.94184 ° N, 93.10426 ° W

Did You Know?
The family's daughter was married in the house's parlor in 1875.

Cathedral of St. Paul

The Cathedral of St. Paul is a church building loosely inspired by St. Peter's Basilica in Rome. The building includes a copper dome on the inside. Many of the statues and art pieces throughout the cathedral date back to its construction in 1915.

The cathedral is listed as the National Shrine of the Apostle Paul by the Vatican. The venue hosts art pieces illustrating the life and death of Saint Paul. You will also find a stone from the wall that surrounds Paul's tomb. The cathedral also has two pipe organs, with more than four thousand combined pipes between the two.

Best Time to Visit:
The church hosts daily masses in the morning, although the weekend masses are the most popular.

Pass/Permit/Fees:
The cathedral accepts donations from all people.

Closest City or Town:
St. Paul

Physical Address:
239 Selby Ave, St. Paul, MN 55102

GPS Coordinates:
44.94699 ° N, 93.10916 ° W

Did You Know?
The city of St. Paul took its name from Paul the Apostle in the 1840s, a few years before its incorporation in 1854.

Center for Lost Objects

You will find many of the most unique art pieces in Minnesota at the Center for Lost Objects in St. Paul. The center houses a gallery and art studio where people produce distinct works of art out of practically anything from random pieces of jewelry to taxidermy animals.

The center also has a store where people can purchase various art items and trinkets. These include many vintage-inspired designs and furniture products made with an offbeat sense of taste.

Best Time to Visit:
The center hosts art and music performances on weekends.

Pass/Permit/Fees:
You can enter for free, but the prices for items at the center will vary.

Closest City or Town:
St. Paul

Physical Address:
957 7th St W, St. Paul, MN 55102

GPS Coordinates:
44.92791 ° N, 93.12682 ° W

Did You Know?
The center also houses monthly figure drawing sessions where people can draw a model draped on one of the unusual items on display here. These include awkward pieces of furniture or rugs made from former animals.

Como Park Zoo & Conservatory

The Como Park Zoo in St. Paul houses many exotic animals, including primates, large cats, and African hoofed animals. There is also a polar bear exhibit at the zoo along with the Marjorie McNeely Conservatory, a 1915 greenhouse with multiple indoor gardens. The Palm Dome houses more than 150 palm species. The conservatory also has a Bonsai garden, a fern room, and a butterfly garden. The zoo and conservatory are among part of the many attractions found around Como Park including a small amusement park for children, a paddleboat station near Lake Como, and a golf course.

Best Time to Visit:
Visit during the summertime to enjoy all the activities.

Pass/Permit/Fees:
There is no admission for entry, but a $3 donation for adults and a $2 donation for kids is encouraged.

Closest City or Town:
St. Paul

Physical Address:
1225 Estabrook Dr, St. Paul, MN 55103

GPS Coordinates:
44.98319 ° N, 93.15349 ° W

Did You Know?
The City of St. Paul owns the land that the zoo and conservatory are on. The city acquired the land in 1873, and it has expanded from 300 acres to nearly 750 acres over the years.

Fort Snelling

Fort Snelling is an old American military fort overlooking the Mississippi and Minnesota Rivers in St. Paul. The fort was built in the 1820s and was essential to the formation of Minnesota as a state. Fort Snelling was used as a training site for many American troops, including ones who served in the Civil War and the Dakota War. The venue continued to operate as a military base until it was decommissioned in 1946. You can visit Fort Snelling and see what the area looked like during the Civil War, including the round tower and the old barracks inside the property. The site also hosts historical reenactments throughout the season.

Best Time to Visit:
The fort has extended visiting hours from June to August.

Pass/Permit/Fees:
Admission is $8 for all people.

Closest City or Town:
St. Paul

Physical Address:
200 Tower Ave, St. Paul, MN 55111

GPS Coordinates:
44.89303 ° N, 93.18071 ° W

Did You Know?
The fort grounds also feature a chapel used for worship purposes. The chapel was originally used by military members, but it is now open to the public for weekly masses.

F. Scott Fitzgerald House

F. Scott Fitzgerald was born in St. Paul and lived in a house on Summit Avenue in the city in the 1910s. He wrote his first novel This Side of Paradise in this house.

Today you can see the F. Scott Fitzgerald House from the outside. The house has a Victorian design witharched windows and a two-story bay window at the front. The design is believed to have been the inspiration for the locations of some of Fitzgerald's books.

Best Time to Visit:
You can walk up to the house any time of the year.

Pass/Permit/Fees:
You can only view the house from the outside. The place does not offer tours.

Closest City or Town:
St. Paul

Physical Address:
599 Summit Ave, St. Paul, MN 55102

GPS Coordinates:
44.94153 ° N, 93.12530 ° W

Did You Know?
While writing This Side of Paradise, Fitzgerald would often go on the balcony outside the third floor of the building to smoke.

Gibbs Museum of Pioneer and Dakotah Life

You can explore pioneer life at the Gibbs Museum in the St. Paul suburb of Falcon Heights. The Ramsey County Historical Society operates many reenactments of pioneer life with costumed performers showing farming activities and working at the sod house. The museum also has a one-room schoolhouse. The property is a recreation of the old schoolhouses used in the state in the nineteenth century. You'll also learn about how the Dakotah band of Native Americans would stop in the area during their annual northern migration for hunting and fishing.

Best Time to Visit:
The museum hosts many programs and events showcasing the history of the area.

Pass/Permit/Fees:
Admission is free, although donations are accepted.

Closest City or Town:
St. Paul

Physical Address:
2097 Larpenteur Ave W, St. Paul, MN 55113

GPS Coordinates:
44.99423 ° N, 93.18731 ° W

Did You Know?
The turtle garden at the museum is based on a medicine teaching garden used by the Dakotah people.

James J. Hill House

Railroad executive James J. Hill lived in an 1891 Romanesque mansion in St. Paul until he died in 1916. You can visit his old residence today, as the James J. Hill House is open for tourists.

The house is a Gilded Age property that for years was the highlight of St. Paul. The first floor has an art gallery, a pipe organ, and Hill's office. The top floor features his bedroom and separate rooms for his five daughters, and the third floor has rooms for his three sons. A gymnasium room and a servant's quarters are also inside the house. Many of these rooms have been refurbished to their original 1891 state.

Best Time to Visit:
The house is open from Thursdays to Sundays each week.

Pass/Permit/Fees:
Admission is $12 for adults and $8 for kids.

Closest City or Town:
St. Paul

Physical Address:
240 Summit Ave, St. Paul, MN 55102

GPS Coordinates:
44.94515 ° N, 93.10896 ° W

Did You Know?
The property featured a hybrid power system that combined gas and electric lighting, although the place did not have any electrical outlets when it was first built.

Landmark Center

The Landmark Center in St. Paul is a Romanesque building that was completed in 1901 as the state's post office and courthouse. The outside has two towers with a clock in one, and it features a pink granite surface.

The center houses many art exhibits and historical displays of life in Minnesota. There is also a theater space for performing arts events. Many of the events are near the five-story courtyard that operates as the focal point of the center.

Best Time to Visit:
You can learn more about what events are at the Landmark Center by visiting landmarkcenter.org. The center's event schedule is always changing.

Pass/Permit/Fees:
While entrance to the center is free in some situations, it may cost extra to attend certain events.

Closest City or Town:
St. Paul

Physical Address:
75 W 5th St, St. Paul, MN 55102

GPS Coordinates:
44.94581 ° N, 93.09711 ° W

Did You Know?
The design of the Landmark Center is like the layout of the Old Post Office in Washington, D.C.

Minnesota State Capitol Building

The Minnesota State Capitol Building in St. Paul is an early-twentieth-century Beaux-Arts building with a design loosely inspired by the United States Capitol. The building houses the state's House of Representatives and Senate, plus it holds the offices of the governor and attorney general. The Capitol features bronze sculptures on the outside and a self-supported marble dome on the inside. You will find twelve marble eagles around the dome, plus many painted murals dating to 1905 on display.

Best Time to Visit:
The Capitol is open throughout the year but may be closed at times due to governmental activities. Visit mnhs.org/capitol to see when it is closed.

Pass/Permit/Fees:
Tours are free, with some showcasing the golden horses outside the Capitol roof.

Closest City or Town:
St. Paul

Physical Address:
75 Rev Dr Martin Luther King Jr Blvd, St. Paul, MN 55155

GPS Coordinates:
44.95524 ° N, 93.10230 ° W

Did You Know?
White marble from Georgia was used in the construction of the Capitol. While granite from Minnesota could have been used, it was decided that the darker granite color would have been too depressing.

Science Museum of Minnesota

The Science Museum of Minnesota is a historic natural history and science museum in St. Paul. It was formed in 1907 and explores the history and evolution of Minnesota. The venue has many replicated dinosaur skeletons, while the Human Body Gallery features exhibits on the many tissues that make up the body. The museum offers exhibits on the evolution of the Mississippi River and how the Dakota and Ojibwe people moved through the state. There's also a large-screen theater that can convert into a rotatable dome for massive viewing events.

Best Time to Visit:
The museum hosts a few special exhibits each year, which are listed on their website.

Pass/Permit/Fees:
Admission is $19 for adults and $12 for kids.

Closest City or Town:
St. Paul

Physical Address:
120 W Kellogg Blvd, St. Paul, MN 55102

GPS Coordinates:
44.94259 ° N, 93.09875 ° W

Did You Know?
The Museum of Questionable Medical Devices is in the Human Body Gallery at the museum. This section features a collection of pseudoscience and quackery items, including a phrenology machine.

The Nook Basement

The Nook is a popular dive bar in St. Paul that prepares many burgers, including the cheese-stuffed Juicy Lucy burger. But the most unique part of the Nook is its bowling alley in the basement. The Ranham Bowling Center is plastered in dollar bills. People who visit the bowling alley will take dollar bills and post them on the ceiling or the walls. The Nook provides markers so people can write messages on their bills. The feature has become a popular attraction among travelers, as about $16,000 worth of dollar bills have been scattered all over the basement.

Best Time to Visit:
The Nook is open until eleven pm every night.

Pass/Permit/Fees:
The cost to bowl in the basement varies throughout the day. The place offers daytime bowling for $10 per hour, or you can rent a lane for two hours for $50 at night. Individual games are also open for $5 each.

Closest City or Town:
St. Paul

Physical Address:
492 Hamline Ave S, St. Paul, MN 55116

GPS Coordinates:
44.92664 ° N, 93.15667 ° W

Did You Know?
It is unclear as to why people started posting dollar bills all around the Nook's basement.

Glacial Pothole Trail, Interstate State Park

The Glacial Pothole Trail at the Interstate State Park on the border with Wisconsin is scattered with many massive potholes. These potholes were formed by glaciers, as the water would often descend downhill and in some cases would cause gravel and other items to slip into a stream. One of the potholes on the trail is the Bottomless Pit, the world's deepest explored pothole. The hole is about sixty feet deep and ten feet wide. You'll find four miles of trail around the park. Nine more miles of trail are on the Wisconsin side.

Best Time to Visit:
The winter season is a fun time to visit, as you can see the icicles forming throughout the trees and rock formations.

Pass/Permit/Fees:
You can visit for free, but it costs extra to reserve a camping site or to rent a canoe or kayak.

Closest City or Town:
Taylors Falls

Physical Address:
307 Milltown Rd, Taylors Falls, MN 55084

GPS Coordinates:
45.39540 ° N, 92.66617 ° W

Did You Know?
Many of the glacial potholes that were formed around the area date back to at least 12,000 years.

Interstate Park

Most of Interstate Park is in Wisconsin, with about 1,300 acres of land. But you will also find about 300 acres of Interstate Park land in Minnesota in Taylors Falls. The Minnesota side of Interstate Park is on the St. Croix River and has many glacial potholes formed over thousands of years.

Interstate Park's landscape is marked by the remnants of many basaltic lava flows from nearly a billion years ago. You'll also find Folsom Island at the midway point of the park as it stands out in the St. Croix River.

Best Time to Visit:
The park is the most comfortable to visit in the summer.

Pass/Permit/Fees:
Admission is free, but it costs money to rent a canoe or kayak to go around the waterways.

Closest City or Town:
Taylors Falls

Physical Address:
307 Milltown Rd, Taylors Falls, MN 55084

GPS Coordinates:
45.40109 ° N, 92.65159 ° W

Did You Know?
Look for the Old Man of the Dalles formation when looking around the cliffs near the water, a face-shaped formation found near the top area.

Lake Vermilion

Lake Vermilion is a northern lake that covers nearly 39,000 acres with multiple boat launching areas around the southern end. You can take a boat to one of the more than 350 islands scattered throughout the landscape. The Bois Forte Band of Chippewa operates its reservation on the southern end of the lake. The band also operates the Fortune Bay Resort Casino on reservation grounds. The Vermilion Dam connects to the Vermilion River that leads north towards Ontario.

Best Time to Visit:
Most of the resorts here are open during the summer season.

Pass/Permit/Fees:
Fishing licenses are required to fish Lake Vermilion.

Closest City or Town:
Tower

Physical Address:
8450 Vermilion Dr, Cook, MN 55723

GPS Coordinates:
47.81350 ° N, 92.30308 ° W

Did You Know?
You can reach Trout Lake to the north by going through Pine Creek or by docking at the southern end of the Trout Lake Portage.

3M Birthplace Museum

The 3M Birthplace Museum in Two Harbors is where the Minnesota Mining and Manufacturing Corporation was formed in 1902. The building was the original office for the corporation, which focused on studying and creating practical applications for minerals found in the area. Many of the original documents focusing on the formation of the company are on display here. The museum highlights the early days of 3M. It includes stories about how the company's many famous products were tested and developed. You'll find many old prototypes of some 3M products here, including the company's sandpaper products, Post-It® notes, and Scotch™ tape.

Best Time to Visit:
The museum is open throughout the year.

Pass/Permit/Fees:
Admission is $5 for everyone, but 3M employees can enter for free.

Closest City or Town:
Two Harbors

Physical Address:
203 Waterfront Dr, Two Harbors, MN 55616

GPS Coordinates:
47.02093 ° N, 91.67120 ° W

Did You Know?
Many of these products came from failed experiments in other technologies, including a failed attempt to make glue which resulted in the Post-It® note.

Iona's Beach

Iona's Beach is a little different from most other beaches around Minnesota. This beach overlooking Lake Superior near Two Harbors has a shore covered in pink rocks. The rocks also make a soft singing-like sound as the tide arrives. The waves will push the rocks around, creating a bell-like sound as the stones resettle. The pink rocks come from a rhyolite cliff as they have fallen over the years.

Best Time to Visit:
The daytime is a better time to visit, as the rocks are more visible, and the water will be more likely to crash into the shoreline.

Pass/Permit/Fees:
While the beach is open for free, it is on a scientific research site. Therefore, you cannot collect any rocks or other items from the site. The area is also not available for boating, fishing, or other recreational activities, although it is popular enough for traditional observation.

Closest City or Town:
Two Harbors

Physical Address:
3548 MN-61, Two Harbors, MN 55616

GPS Coordinates:
47.16762 ° N, 91.42152 ° W

Did You Know?
Iona's Beach is named after Iona Lind, the owner of a resort that was once in the local area.

Split Rock Lighthouse State Park

You will find the iconic Split Rock Lighthouse at the state park that shares its name in Two Harbors. The lighthouse appears on a rocky cliff overlooking Lake Superior. You can hike down the trail to the northeast to reach the lighthouse.

There are a few spots where you can take photos of the lighthouse as you get closer. You'll also find a pump house not far from the lighthouse. The park also features a small beach to the south near Ellingson Island. The Corundum Point outlook area is also to the south.

Best Time to Visit:
The beacon atop the lighthouse is lit on November 10 of each year. The lighting honors the wreck of the *SS Edmund Fitzgerald*.

Pass/Permit/Fees:
It is free to visit the area.

Closest City or Town:
Two Harbors

Physical Address:
3755 Split Rock Lighthouse Rd, Two Harbors, MN 55616

GPS Coordinates:
47.19947 ° N, 91.37486 ° W

Did You Know?
You can go scuba diving off the park shore to see the *SS Madeira* wreck.

Great River Bluffs State Park

The Great River Bluffs State Park in the southeastern part of the state has many steep bluffs overlooking the Mississippi River, many of which climb nearly 500 feet above the river.

The park houses a few hiking trails, with some going through sites used for scientific research and studies. There are also a few goat prairies around the area that are extremely steep.

Best Time to Visit:
The summer season is an ideal time to visit the area.

Pass/Permit/Fees:
You can visit the area for free.

Closest City or Town:
Winona

Physical Address:
43605 Kipp Dr, Winona, MN 55987

GPS Coordinates:
43.94898 ° N, 91.40503 ° W

Did You Know?
Some of the rock formations around the park include dolomite banks near the river. Dolomite is noteworthy for resisting erosion.

Proper Planning

With this guide, you are well on your way to properly planning a marvelous adventure. When you plan your travels, you should become familiar with the area, save any maps to your phone for access without internet, and bring plenty of water—especially during the summer months. Depending on which adventure you choose, you will also want to bring snacks or even a lunch. For younger children, you should do your research and find destinations that best suit your family's needs. Remember to plan when and where to get gas, local lodgings, and food. We've done our best to group these destinations based on nearby towns and cities to help make planning easier.

Dangerous Wildlife

There are several dangerous animals and insects you may encounter while hiking. With a good dose of caution and awareness, you can explore safely. Here are steps you can take to keep yourself and your loved ones safe from dangerous flora and fauna while exploring:

- Keep to the established trails.
- Do not look under rocks, leaves, or sticks.
- Keep hands and feet out of small crawl spaces, bushes, covered areas, or crevices.
- Wear long sleeves and pants to keep arms and legs protected.
- Keep your distance should you encounter any dangerous wildlife or plants.

Limited Cell Service

Do not rely on cell service for navigation or emergencies. Always have a map with you and let someone know where you are and how long you intend to be gone, just in case.

First Aid Information

Always travel with a first aid kit in case of emergencies.

Here are items you should be certain to include in your primary first aid kit:

- Nitrile gloves
- Blister care products
- Band-Aids in multiple sizes and waterproof type
- Ace wrap and athletic tape
- Alcohol wipes and antibiotic ointment
- Irrigation syringe
- Tweezers, nail clippers, trauma shears, safety pins
- Small zip-lock bags for contaminated trash

It is recommended to also keep a secondary first aid kit, especially when hiking, for more serious injuries or medical emergencies. Items in this should include:

- Blood clotting sponges
- Sterile gauze pads
- Trauma pads
- Second-skin/burn treatment

- Triangular bandages/sling
- Butterfly strips
- Tincture of benzoin
- Medications (ibuprofen, acetaminophen, antihistamine, aspirin, etc.)
- Thermometer
- CPR mask
- Wilderness medicine handbook
- Antivenom

There is much more to explore, but this is a great start.

For information on all national parks, visit https://www.nps.gov/index.htm .

This site will give you information on up-to-date entrance fees and how to purchase a park pass for unlimited access to national and state parks. It will also introduce you to all of the trails at each park.

Always check before you travel to destinations to make sure there are no closures. Some hiking trails close when there is heavy rain or snow in the area and other parks close parts of their land for the migration of wildlife. Attractions may change their hours or temporarily shut down for various reasons. Check the websites for the most up-to-date information.

Made in the USA
Monee, IL
19 December 2023

49936230R00077